50 STATES 5000 IDEAS

JOURNAL

NATIONAL GEOGRAPHIC

WASHINGTON, D.C.

THIS JOURNAL BELONGS TO:

_____

_____

_____

CONTENTS

WASHINGTON

MONTANA

NORTH DAKOTA

MINNESOTA

OREGON

IDAHO

SOUTH DAKOTA

WYOMING

MIDWEST

WEST

NEBRASKA

IOWA

NEVADA

UTAH

CALIFORNIA

COLORADO

KANSAS

MISSOURI

ARIZONA

OKLAHOMA

NEW MEXICO

ARKANSAS

SOUTHWEST

TEXAS

ALASKA

UNITED STATES

NORTHERN MARIANA IS. (TERRITORY)

GUAM (TERR.)   **AMERICAN SAMOA (TERR.)**

MAINE

VT.
N.H.

MICHIGAN

WISCONSIN

NEW YORK   MASS.

CONN. R.I.

NORTHEAST

PENNSYLVANIA

NEW JERSEY

OHIO

MD.

DELAWARE

ILLINOIS   INDIANA

DISTRICT OF COLUMBIA (TERR.)

WEST VIRGINIA

VIRGINIA

KENTUCKY

NORTH CAROLINA

TENNESSEE

SOUTHEAST   SOUTH CAROLINA

GEORGIA

MISSISSIPPI   ALABAMA

LOUISIANA

FLORIDA

HAWAI'I

PUERTO RICO (TERR.)

U.S. VIRGIN ISLANDS (TERR.)

PLACES VISITED

- ☐ Alabama
- ☐ Alaska
- ☐ American Samoa
- ☐ Arizona
- ☐ Arkansas
- ☐ California
- ☐ Colorado
- ☐ Connecticut
- ☐ Delaware
- ☐ District of Columbia
- ☐ Florida
- ☐ Georgia
- ☐ Guam
- ☐ Hawaii
- ☐ Idaho
- ☐ Illinois
- ☐ Indiana
- ☐ Iowa
- ☐ Kansas
- ☐ Kentucky
- ☐ Louisiana
- ☐ Maine
- ☐ Maryland
- ☐ Massachusetts
- ☐ Michigan
- ☐ Minnesota
- ☐ Mississippi
- ☐ Missouri

- ☐ Montana
- ☐ Nebraska
- ☐ Nevada
- ☐ New Hampshire
- ☐ New Jersey
- ☐ New Mexico
- ☐ New York
- ☐ North Carolina
- ☐ North Dakota
- ☐ Northern Mariana Islands
- ☐ Ohio
- ☐ Oklahoma
- ☐ Oregon
- ☐ Pennsylvania
- ☐ Puerto Rico
- ☐ Rhode Island
- ☐ South Carolina
- ☐ South Dakota
- ☐ Tennessee
- ☐ Texas
- ☐ U.S. Virgin Islands
- ☐ Utah
- ☐ Vermont
- ☐ Virginia
- ☐ Washington
- ☐ West Virginia
- ☐ Wisconsin
- ☐ Wyoming

Alabama

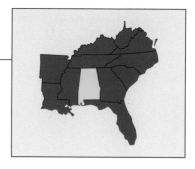

STATE CAPITAL: Montgomery | **POPULATION:** 5,074,296 *(July 2022)*
STATE NICKNAME: The Heart of Dixie | **YEAR OF STATEHOOD:** 1819
FUN FACT: Montgomery was the center of the American civil rights movement.

MAIN ATTRACTIONS:

CITIES: Birmingham, Florala, Florence, Gulf Shores, Huntsville, Mobile, Montgomery, Tuscaloosa, Winfield

LANDSCAPES: Alabama's Gulf Coast, Appalachian Mountains, Black Warrior River, Florala City Park, Gulf State Park, Little River Canyon National Preserve, Lookout Mountain

POINTS OF INTEREST: Alabama Aviation Hall of Fame, Alabama Gulf Coast Zoo, Alabama Jazz Hall of Fame, Barber Vintage Motorsports Museum, Birmingham Civil Rights District, Birmingham Civil Rights Institute, Bryant-Denny Stadium, Frank Lloyd Wright's Rosenbaum House, Mobile Carnival Museum, NASA's Marshall Space Flight Center, Southern Museum of Flight, Tuskegee Airmen National Historic Site, U.S. Space & Rocket Center, U.S.S. *Alabama* Battleship Memorial Park, Vulcan Park and Museum

DATE VISITED:

WEATHER:

WHERE I WENT:

WHERE I STAYED:

WHO I WENT WITH:

FAVORITE MOMENT:

BEST DRIVING OR WALKING TOUR:

WHAT I'D RECOMMEND:

TIPS TO FRIENDS/FAMILY:

WHAT I WISH I KNEW BEFORE GOING:

WHAT WAS THE FIRST THING I NOTICED WHEN I ARRIVED?

MY FAVORITE PART OF THE VISIT WAS . . .

HOW I SPENT MY TIME THERE:

WHAT WOULD I DO IF I GO BACK?

WHAT IS SOMETHING I LEARNED THERE?

MY TOP THREE FAVORITE ACTIVITIES WERE . . .

1.

2.

3

MY TRIP WAS

10

JAN		FEB		MAR		APR		MAY		JUN		JUL		AUG		SEP		OCT		NOV		DEC
1	2	3	4	5	6	7	8	9	10	11	12	13	14	15	16	17	18	19	20	21	22	23	24	25	26	27	28	29	30	31

Alaska

STATE CAPITAL: Juneau | **POPULATION:** 733,583 *(July 2022)*
STATE NICKNAME: The Last Frontier | **YEAR OF STATEHOOD:** 1959
FUN FACT: Denali National Park & Preserve is the only U.S. national park in which sled dogs are used to patrol the area.

MAIN ATTRACTIONS:

CITIES: Anchorage, Fairbanks, Homer, Juneau, Lake Hood, Seward

LANDSCAPES: Alaska Range, Arctic National Wildlife Refuge, Bering Land Bridge National Preserve, Cape Krusenstern National Monument, Chugach State Park, Denali National Park & Preserve, Gates of the Arctic National Park & Preserve, Glacier Bay National Park & Preserve, Iditarod National Historic Trail, Inside Passage, Kenai Fjords National Park, Kobuk Valley National Park, Kodiak National Wildlife Refuge, Lake Clark National Park & Preserve, Mendenhall Glacier, Portage Glacier, Tongass National Forest, Tracy Arm Fjord, Wrangell–St. Elias National Park & Preserve

POINTS OF INTEREST: AJ Mine Gastineau Mill Tour, Alaska Native Heritage Center, Alaska SeaLife Center, Goldbelt Tram, Ketchikan's Totem Heritage Center, Last Chance Mining Museum, Running Reindeer Ranch, Wynn Nature Center

DATE VISITED:

WEATHER:

WHERE I WENT:

WHERE I STAYED:

WHO I WENT WITH:

FAVORITE MOMENT:

BEST DRIVING OR WALKING TOUR:

WHAT I'D RECOMMEND:

TIPS TO FRIENDS/FAMILY:

WHAT I WISH I KNEW BEFORE GOING:

WHAT WAS THE FIRST THING I NOTICED WHEN I ARRIVED?

MY FAVORITE PART OF THE VISIT WAS . . .

HOW I SPENT MY TIME THERE:

WHAT WOULD I DO IF I GO BACK?

WHAT IS SOMETHING I LEARNED THERE?

MY TOP THREE FAVORITE ACTIVITIES WERE . . .

1.

2.

3

MY TRIP WAS

JAN	FEB	MAR	APR	MAY	JUN	JUL	AUG	SEP	OCT	NOV	DEC
1 2 3	4 5 6	7 8 9	10 11 12	13 14 15	16 17	18 19 20	21 22	23 24 25	26 27	28 29	30 31

....

....

....

....

....

....

....

....

....

....

....

....

....

....

....

....

....

....

....

....

....

....

....

American Samoa

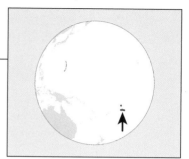

TERRITORY CAPITAL: Pago Pago | **POPULATION:** 44,620 *(April 2023)*
TERRITORY NICKNAME: Motu O Fiafiaga (Island of Paradise) | **YEAR OF U.S. TERRITORYHOOD:** 1900 (Tutuila) | **FUN FACT:** The only U.S. national park located south of the Equator is the National Park of American Samoa.

MAIN ATTRACTIONS:

ISLANDS: Aunuʻu, Ofu, Olosega, Pago Pago, Rose Atoll, Swains Island, Taʻu, Tutuila

CITIES: Aūa, Fagatogo, Faleniu, Leone, Mapusagafou, Pago Pago, Tāfuna, Vaitogi

LANDSCAPES: Alofaaga Blowholes, Aunuʻu Island, Fagatele Bay National Marine Sanctuary, Fogamaʻa Bay and Crater, Matafao Peak, Mount ʻAlava, National Park of American Samoa, Ofu Beach, To Sua ocean trench, Utulei Beach Park

POINTS OF INTEREST: Jean P. Haydon Museum, Massacre Bay, National Marine Sanctuary of American Samoa, Pago Pago Harbor, Tauese P.F. Sunia Ocean Center, Tramway Memorial & Lookout

---

DATE VISITED:

WEATHER:

WHERE I WENT:

WHERE I STAYED:

WHO I WENT WITH:

FAVORITE MOMENT

BEST DRIVING OR WALKING TOUR:

WHAT I'D RECOMMEND:

TIPS TO FRIENDS/FAMILY:

WHAT I WISH I KNEW BEFORE GOING:

WHAT WAS THE FIRST THING I NOTICED WHEN I ARRIVED?

MY FAVORITE PART OF THE VISIT WAS . . .

HOW I SPENT MY TIME THERE:

WHAT WOULD I DO IF I GO BACK?

WHAT IS SOMETHING I LEARNED THERE?

MY TOP THREE FAVORITE ACTIVITIES WERE . . .

1.

2.

3

MY TRIP WAS

/10

JAN   FEB   MAR   APR   MAY   JUN   JUL   AUG   SEP   OCT   NOV   DEC
1   2   3   4   5   6   7   8   9   10   11   12   13   14   15   16   17   18   19   20   21   22   23   24   25   26   27   28   29   30   31

Arizona

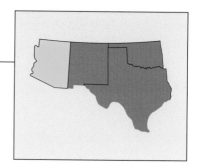

STATE CAPITAL: Phoenix | **POPULATION:** 7,359,197 *(July 2022)*
STATE NICKNAME: The Grand Canyon State | **YEAR OF STATE-HOOD:** 1912 | **FUN FACT:** The chimichanga was invented by Monica Flin at a restaurant in downtown Tucson in the 1920s.

MAIN ATTRACTIONS:

CITIES: Flagstaff, Jerome, Lake Havasu City, Phoenix, Prescott, Scottsdale, Sedona, Tombstone, Tucson, Williams, Yuma

LANDSCAPES: Bearizona Wildlife Park, Cabeza Prieta National Wildlife Refuge, Camelback Mountain, Canyon de Chelly National Monument, Chiricahua Mountains, Colorado River, Grand Canyon National Park, Lake Havasu, Monument Valley Navajo Tribal Park, Organ Pipe Cactus Biosphere Reserve, Organ Pipe Cactus National Monument, Painted Desert, Petrified Forest National Park, Pipe Spring National Monument, Saguaro National Park, Sonoran Desert, Sunset Crater Volcano National Monument, Verde River, Verde Valley, Vermilion Cliffs National Monument

POINTS OF INTEREST: Arizona-Sonora Desert Museum, Desert Botanical Garden, Heard Museum, Lowell Observatory, Meteor Crater, Musical Instrument Museum, Pima Air & Space Museum, San Xavier del Bac Mission, Taliesin West, Tucson Museum of Art

---

DATE VISITED:

WEATHER:

WHERE I WENT:

WHERE I STAYED:

WHO I WENT WITH:

FAVORITE MOMENT:

BEST DRIVING OR WALKING TOUR:

WHAT I'D RECOMMEND:

TIPS TO FRIENDS/FAMILY:

WHAT I WISH I KNEW BEFORE GOING:

WHAT WAS THE FIRST THING I NOTICED WHEN I ARRIVED?

MY FAVORITE PART OF THE VISIT WAS . . .

HOW I SPENT MY TIME THERE:

WHAT WOULD I DO IF I GO BACK?

WHAT IS SOMETHING I LEARNED THERE?

MY TOP THREE FAVORITE ACTIVITIES WERE . . .

1.

2.

3

MY TRIP WAS

10

JAN   FEB   MAR   APR   MAY   JUN   JUL   AUG   SEP   OCT   NOV   DEC

1 2 3 4 5 6 7 8 9 10 11 12 13 14 15 16 17 18 19 20 21 22 23 24 25 26 27 28 29 30 31

Arkansas

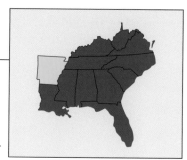

STATE CAPITAL: Little Rock | **POPULATION:** 3,045,637 *(July 2022)*
STATE NICKNAME: The Natural State | **YEAR OF STATEHOOD:** 1836
FUN FACT: The reserve that protects Hot Springs National Park is the oldest participant in the National Park System, designated 40 years before Yellowstone.

MAIN ATTRACTIONS:

CITIES: Bentonville, Eureka Springs, Fayetteville, Fort Smith, Hope, Hot Springs, Little Rock, Mountain View, Washington

LANDSCAPES: Arkansas Delta, Blanchard Springs Caverns, Historic Washington State Park, Hot Springs National Park, Lake Chicot State Park, MacArthur Park, Magnetic Mountain, Mississippi River, Ouachita Mountains, Ozark–St. Francis National Forests, Pea Ridge National Military Park, Petit Jean State Park

POINTS OF INTEREST: Buckstaff Bathhouse, Christ of the Ozarks statue, Clinton Presidential Center, Crystal Bridges Museum of American Art, ESSE Purse Museum, Fort Smith National Historic Site, Heifer Village, Hot Springs Mountain Tower, Little Rock Central High School National Historic Site, Miss Laura's Social Club, Museum of Discovery, Old Mill, Turpentine Creek Wildlife Refuge, William J. Clinton Presidential Library & Museum, Witt Stephens Jr. Central Arkansas Nature Center

DATE VISITED:

WEATHER:

WHERE I WENT:

WHERE I STAYED:

WHO I WENT WITH:

FAVORITE MOMENT:

BEST DRIVING OR WALKING TOUR:

WHAT I'D RECOMMEND:

TIPS TO FRIENDS/FAMILY:

WHAT I WISH I KNEW BEFORE GOING:

WHAT WAS THE FIRST THING I NOTICED WHEN I ARRIVED?

MY FAVORITE PART OF THE VISIT WAS . . .

HOW I SPENT MY TIME THERE:

WHAT WOULD I DO IF I GO BACK?

WHAT IS SOMETHING I LEARNED THERE?

MY TOP THREE FAVORITE ACTIVITIES WERE . . .

1.

2.

3

MY TRIP WAS

/10

JAN	FEB	MAR	APR	MAY	JUN	JUL	AUG	SEP	OCT	NOV	DEC
1 2 3	4 5 6	7 8 9	10 11 12	13 14 15	16 17	18 19 20	21 22	23 24 25	26 27	28 29	30 31

....

....

....

....

....

....

....

....

....

....

....

....

....

....

....

....

....

....

....

....

....

....

California

STATE CAPITAL: Sacramento | **POPULATION:** 39,029,342 *(July 2022)*
STATE NICKNAME: The Golden State | **YEAR OF STATEHOOD:** 1850
FUN FACT: California holds the record for most state capital changes with a total of seven, including Sacramento before and after San Francisco.

MAIN ATTRACTIONS:

CITIES: Anaheim, Long Beach, Los Angeles, Malibu, Napa, Palm Springs, Palo Alto, Pasadena, Sacramento, San Diego, San Francisco, San Jose, Santa Barbara, Santa Monica, Sonoma

LANDSCAPES: Big Sur, Cascade Range, Death Valley National Park, Echo Park, Gold Country, Golden Gate Park, Joshua Tree National Park, Lake Tahoe, Mojave Desert, Pacific Coast Highway, Redwood National and State Parks, Sequoia & Kings Canyon National Park, Sierra Nevada mountains, Yosemite National Park

POINTS OF INTEREST: The Broad, Disneyland, Getty Center, Golden Gate Bridge, GRAMMY Museum, Hollywood Boulevard, Hotel del Coronado, Los Angeles County Museum of Art (LACMA), Mission San Juan Capistrano, Museum of Contemporary Art (MOCA), Palace of Fine Arts, *Queen Mary,* Walt Disney Concert Hall

DATE VISITED:

WEATHER:

WHERE I WENT:

WHERE I STAYED:

WHO I WENT WITH:

FAVORITE MOMENT:

BEST DRIVING OR WALKING TOUR:

WHAT I'D RECOMMEND:

TIPS TO FRIENDS/FAMILY:

WHAT I WISH I KNEW BEFORE GOING:

WHAT WAS THE FIRST THING I NOTICED WHEN I ARRIVED?

MY FAVORITE PART OF THE VISIT WAS . . .

HOW I SPENT MY TIME THERE:

WHAT WOULD I DO IF I GO BACK?

WHAT IS SOMETHING I LEARNED THERE?

MY TOP THREE FAVORITE ACTIVITIES WERE . . .

1.

2.

3

MY TRIP WAS

JAN	FEB	MAR	APR	MAY	JUN	JUL	AUG	SEP	OCT	NOV	DEC

1 2 3 4 5 6 7 8 9 10 11 12 13 14 15 16 17 18 19 20 21 22 23 24 25 26 27 28 29 30 31

....

....

....

....

....

....

....

....

....

....

....

....

....

....

....

....

....

....

....

....

....

....

Colorado

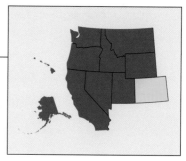

STATE CAPITAL: Denver | **POPULATION:** 5,839,926 *(July 2022)*
STATE NICKNAME: The Centennial State | **YEAR OF STATEHOOD:** 1876
FUN FACT: Denver is perched a mile above sea level.

MAIN ATTRACTIONS:

CITIES: Aspen, Boulder, Breckenridge, Colorado Springs, Denver, Durango, Fort Collins, Georgetown, Manitou Springs, Silver Plume, Silverton, Telluride, Vail

LANDSCAPES: Bear Creek Falls, Black Canyon of the Gunnison National Park, Cave of the Winds Mountain Park, Colorado National Monument, Dinosaur National Monument, Garden of the Gods, Holy Cross Wilderness, Mesa Verde National Park, North Cheyenne Cañon Park, Pikes Peak, Rocky Mountain National Park, Royal Gorge, White River National Forest

POINTS OF INTEREST: Ashcroft Ghost Town, Aspen Art Museum, Black American West Museum & Heritage Center, Colorado Snowsports Museum, Denver Botanic Gardens, Denver Zoo, Elitch Gardens Theme & Water Park, Fort Collins Trolley, Miramont Castle Museum, National Museum of World War II Aviation, Royal Gorge Bridge, St. Elmo Ghost Town, U.S. Air Force Academy, Wheeler Opera House

DATE VISITED:

WEATHER:

WHERE I WENT:

WHERE I STAYED:

WHO I WENT WITH:

FAVORITE MOMENT:

BEST DRIVING OR WALKING TOUR:

WHAT I'D RECOMMEND:

TIPS TO FRIENDS/FAMILY:

WHAT I WISH I KNEW BEFORE GOING:

WHAT WAS THE FIRST THING I NOTICED WHEN I ARRIVED?

MY FAVORITE PART OF THE VISIT WAS . . .

HOW I SPENT MY TIME THERE:

WHAT WOULD I DO IF I GO BACK?

WHAT IS SOMETHING I LEARNED THERE?

MY TOP THREE FAVORITE ACTIVITIES WERE . . .

1.

2.

3

MY TRIP WAS

JAN   FEB   MAR   APR   MAY   JUN   JUL   AUG   SEP   OCT   NOV   DEC

1 2 3 4 5 6 7 8 9 10 11 12 13 14 15 16 17 18 19 20 21 22 23 24 25 26 27 28 29 30 31

Connecticut

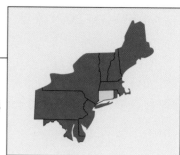

STATE CAPITAL: Hartford | **POPULATION:** 3,626,205 *(July 2022)*
STATE NICKNAME: The Constitution State | **YEAR OF STATEHOOD:** 1788
FUN FACT: Bushnell Park in Hartford is America's first ever municipal park, paid for by the citizens through a popular vote.

MAIN ATTRACTIONS:

CITIES: Bloomfield, Bridgeport, East Haddam, Greenwich, Groton, Guilford, Hartford, Litchfield, Mashantucket, Mystic, New Canaan, New Haven, New London, Old Lyme, Ridgefield, Wilton, Windham, Windsor Locks, Woodstock

LANDSCAPES: East Rock Park, Great Captain Island, Heublein Tower, Island Beach, Long Island Sound, Mill River Park, Talcott Mountain State Park, Thames River

POINTS OF INTEREST: Bushnell Park, Byram Park, Corning Fountain, Fayerweather Island Lighthouse, Five Mile Point Lighthouse, Gillette Castle State Park, Goodspeed Opera House, Haight-Brown Vineyard, Harriet Beecher Stowe Center, Jones Family Farms, Lake Compounce, Mark Twain House & Museum, Mystic Aquarium, New England Air Museum, Philip Johnson's Glass House, Putnam Cottage, Soldier and Sailors Memorial Arch, Spanish-American War Memorial, U.S.S. *Nautilus,* Wadsworth Atheneum Museum of Art, Yale University

DATE VISITED:	WHO I WENT WITH:	WHAT I'D RECOMMEND:
WEATHER:	**FAVORITE MOMENT:**	**TIPS TO FRIENDS/FAMILY:**
WHERE I WENT:		
WHERE I STAYED:	**BEST DRIVING OR WALKING TOUR:**	**WHAT I WISH I KNEW BEFORE GOING:**

WHAT WAS THE FIRST THING I NOTICED WHEN I ARRIVED?

MY FAVORITE PART OF
THE VISIT WAS . . .

HOW I SPENT MY TIME THERE:

WHAT WOULD I DO IF I GO BACK?

WHAT IS SOMETHING I LEARNED THERE?

MY TOP THREE FAVORITE ACTIVITIES WERE . . .

1.

2.

3

MY TRIP WAS

JAN   FEB   MAR   APR   MAY   JUN   JUL   AUG   SEP   OCT   NOV   DEC
1   2   3   4   5   6   7   8   9   10   11   12   13   14   15   16   17   18   19   20   21   22   23   24   25   26   27   28   29   30   31

....

....

....

....

....

....

....

....

....

....

....

....

....

....

....

....

....

....

....

....

Delaware

STATE CAPITAL: Dover | **POPULATION:** 1,018,396 *(July 2022)*
STATE NICKNAME: The First State | **YEAR OF STATEHOOD:** 1787
FUN FACT: New Castle Court House is one of the oldest surviving courthouses in the U.S., originally built in 1732.

MAIN ATTRACTIONS:

CITIES: Brandywine Valley, Chateau Country, Dewey Beach, Dover, Laurel, Lewes, New Castle, Rehoboth Beach, Smyrna, Wilmington

LANDSCAPES: Auburn Valley State Park, Bombay Hook National Wildlife Refuge, Brandywine Creek State Park, Cape Henlopen State Park, Delaware Seashore State Park, Junction & Breakwater Trail, Russell W. Peterson Urban Wildlife Refuge, Trap Pond State Park, Tulip Tree Woods Nature Preserve, Woodlawn Tract

POINTS OF INTEREST: Air Mobility Command Museum, Clear Space Theatre Company, Delaware Children's Museum, Delaware Sports Museum & Hall of Fame, Dogfish Head Craft Brewery, DuPont Environmental Education Center, Fenwick Island, First State Heritage Park, Funland Rehoboth, Grand Opera House, Great Marsh Park, Marshall Steam Museum, Nanticoke Indian Museum, Nemours Estate, Rehoboth Beach Boardwalk, Riverfront Wilmington, Winterthur Museum—Garden & Library

DATE VISITED:	WHO I WENT WITH:	WHAT I'D RECOMMEND:
WEATHER:		
	FAVORITE MOMENT:	**TIPS TO FRIENDS/FAMILY:**
WHERE I WENT:		
	BEST DRIVING OR WALKING TOUR:	**WHAT I WISH I KNEW BEFORE GOING:**
WHERE I STAYED:		

WHAT WAS THE FIRST THING I NOTICED WHEN I ARRIVED?

MY FAVORITE PART OF THE VISIT WAS . . .

HOW I SPENT MY TIME THERE:

WHAT WOULD I DO IF I GO BACK?

WHAT IS SOMETHING I LEARNED THERE?

MY TOP THREE FAVORITE ACTIVITIES WERE . . .

1.

2.

3

MY TRIP WAS

/10

JAN	FEB	MAR	APR	MAY	JUN	JUL	AUG	SEP	OCT	NOV	DEC

1 2 3 4 5 6 7 8 9 10 11 12 13 14 15 16 17 18 19 20 21 22 23 24 25 26 27 28 29 30 31

District of Columbia

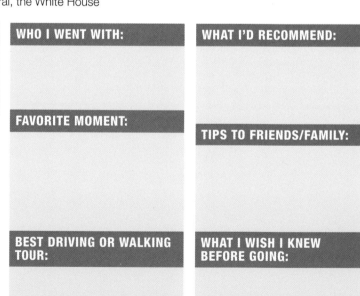

U.S. capital | **POPULATION:** 671,803 *(July 2022)* | **NICKNAME:**
The District | **YEAR ESTABLISHED:** 1790 | **FUN FACT:** Miles of tunnels
run beneath the Capitol but they aren't related to the Metro system—they
allow federal employees to shuttle from one government building to another.

MAIN ATTRACTIONS:

NEIGHBORHOODS: Adams Morgan, Anacostia, Brookland, Capitol Hill, Downtown, Dupont Circle, Foggy Bottom, Georgetown, Ivy City, Logan Circle, Navy Yard, Tenleytown

LANDSCAPES: Capital Crescent Trail, Chesapeake & Ohio Canal Towpath, Rock Creek Park, Tidal Basin

POINTS OF INTEREST: Basilica of the National Shrine of the Immaculate Conception, the Ellipse, Franklin Delano Roosevelt Memorial, Friendship Archway, International Spy Museum, Korean War Veterans Memorial, Lincoln Memorial, Martin Luther King, Jr. Memorial, National Air and Space Museum, National Gallery of Art, National Mall, National Museum of African American History & Culture, National Museum of African Art, National Museum of American History, National Museum of Natural History, National Zoo, Thomas Jefferson Memorial, U.S. Capitol, Washington Monument, Washington National Cathedral, the White House

DATE VISITED:

WEATHER:

WHERE I WENT:

WHERE I STAYED:

WHO I WENT WITH:

FAVORITE MOMENT:

BEST DRIVING OR WALKING TOUR:

WHAT I'D RECOMMEND:

TIPS TO FRIENDS/FAMILY:

WHAT I WISH I KNEW BEFORE GOING:

WHAT WAS THE FIRST THING I NOTICED WHEN I ARRIVED?

MY FAVORITE PART OF
THE VISIT WAS . . .

HOW I SPENT MY TIME THERE:

WHAT WOULD I DO IF I GO BACK?

WHAT IS SOMETHING I LEARNED THERE?

MY TOP THREE FAVORITE ACTIVITIES WERE . . .

1.

2.

3

MY TRIP WAS

/10

JAN		FEB			MAR			APR			MAY			JUN			JUL			AUG			SEP			OCT			NOV			DEC
1	2	3	4	5	6	7	8	9	10	11	12	13	14	15	16	17	18	19	20	21	22	23	24	25	26	27	28	29	30	31

Florida

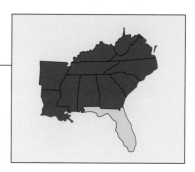

STATE CAPITAL: Tallahassee | **POPULATION:** 22,244,823 *(July 2022)*
STATE NICKNAME: The Sunshine State | **YEAR OF STATEHOOD:** 1845
FUN FACT: Fort Mose in St. Augustine was founded in 1738 and became the first free Black settlement in North America.

MAIN ATTRACTIONS:

CITIES: Cape Canaveral, Daytona Beach, Homestead, Jacksonville, Fort Lauderdale, Key Biscayne, Miami, Naples, Orlando, Panama City, Pensacola, St. Augustine, St. Petersburg, Sarasota, Siesta Key, Tallahassee, Tampa, Tarpon Springs

LANDSCAPES: Biscayne National Park, Camp Helen State Park, Dry Tortugas National Park, Everglades National Park, Florida Keys, Gulf Islands National Seashore, The Nature Conservancy's Disney Wilderness Preserve, Perdido Key, St. Andrews State Park, Virginia Key Beach Park

POINTS OF INTEREST: *American Victory* Ship & Museum, Catty Shack Ranch Wildlife Sanctuary, Charles Hosmer Morse Museum of American Art, Daytona International Speedway, Gatorland, Indian Temple Mound Museum, Little Havana, National Naval Aviation Museum, Orlando Science Center, Pérez Art Museum Miami, Sunshine Skyway Bridge, Universal Studios Florida, Walt Disney World, Ybor City, Zoo Miami

DATE VISITED:

WEATHER:

WHERE I WENT:

WHERE I STAYED:

WHO I WENT WITH:

FAVORITE MOMENT:

BEST DRIVING OR WALKING TOUR:

WHAT I'D RECOMMEND:

TIPS TO FRIENDS/FAMILY:

WHAT I WISH I KNEW BEFORE GOING:

WHAT WAS THE FIRST THING I NOTICED WHEN I ARRIVED?

MY FAVORITE PART OF THE VISIT WAS . . .

HOW I SPENT MY TIME THERE:

WHAT WOULD I DO IF I GO BACK?

WHAT IS SOMETHING I LEARNED THERE?

MY TOP THREE FAVORITE ACTIVITIES WERE . . .

1.

2.

3

MY TRIP WAS

/10

JAN   FEB   MAR   APR   MAY   JUN   JUL   AUG   SEP   OCT   NOV   DEC
1   2   3   4   5   6   7   8   9   10   11   12   13   14   15   16   17   18   19   20   21   22   23   24   25   26   27   28   29   30   31

Georgia

STATE CAPITAL: Atlanta | **POPULATION:** 10,912,876 *(July 2022)*
STATE NICKNAME: The Peach State | **YEAR OF STATEHOOD:** 1788
FUN FACT: The birthplace of the famous Cabbage Patch Kids dolls was at the Babyland General Hospital located in Cleveland, Georgia.

MAIN ATTRACTIONS:

CITIES: Andersonville, Atlanta, Augusta, Blue Ridge, Brunswick, McCaysville, Plains, Savannah, Senoia, Warm Springs, Warner Robins

LANDSCAPES: Chattahoochee-Oconee National Forest, Chattooga River, Cumberland Island National Seashore, Kennesaw Mountain National Battlefield Park, Sapelo Island, Sea Island, Stone Mountain Park, Tallulah Gorge State Park

POINTS OF INTEREST: Augusta Museum of History, Augusta National Golf Club, Centennial Olympic Park, Chippewa Square, Forsyth Park, Georgia Aquarium, Jimmy Carter National Historic Site, Martin Luther King, Jr. National Historical Park, Museum of Aviation, National Center for Civil and Human Rights, Roosevelt's Little White House, Savannah Theatre, Sweet Auburn Historic District, Tybee Island Light Station & Museum

DATE VISITED:

WEATHER:

WHERE I WENT:

WHERE I STAYED:

WHO I WENT WITH:

FAVORITE MOMENT:

BEST DRIVING OR WALKING TOUR:

WHAT I'D RECOMMEND:

TIPS TO FRIENDS/FAMILY:

WHAT I WISH I KNEW BEFORE GOING:

WHAT WAS THE FIRST THING I NOTICED WHEN I ARRIVED?

MY FAVORITE PART OF THE VISIT WAS . . .

HOW I SPENT MY TIME THERE:

WHAT WOULD I DO IF I GO BACK?

WHAT IS SOMETHING I LEARNED THERE?

MY TOP THREE FAVORITE ACTIVITIES WERE . . .

1.

2.

3

MY TRIP WAS

/10

JAN			FEB			MAR			APR			MAY			JUN			JUL			AUG			SEP			OCT			NOV			DEC
1	2	3	4	5	6	7	8	9	10	11	12	13	14	15	16	17	18	19	20	21	22	23	24	25	26	27	28	29	30	31

Guam

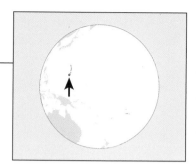

TERRITORY CAPITAL: Hagåtña (Agana) **| POPULATION:** 169,330 *(April 2023)* **| TERRITORY NICKNAME:** Tano y Chamorro (Land of the Chamorro) **| YEAR OF U.S. TERRITORYHOOD:** 1898 **| FUN FACT:** In 1972, an Imperial Japanese Army sergeant was found in the jungles of Guam, having hidden there for nearly 28 years after World War II ended.

MAIN ATTRACTIONS:

CITIES: Dededo, Hagåtña, Inarajan, Tamuning, Umatac

LANDSCAPES: Agfayan Bay, Cocos Island, Governor Joseph Flores Beach Park, Guam National Wildlife Refuge, Inarajan Natural Pool, Mount Bolanos, Mount Lamlam, Shark's Cove Beach, Talofofo Falls, Tumon Bay Marine Preserve

POINTS OF INTEREST: Apra Harbor shipwrecks, Chamorro Village Wednesday Night Market, Chinese Park, Dulce Nombre de Maria Cathedral-Basilica, Fort Nuestra Señora de la Soledad, Fort Santa Agueda, Gef Pa'go Cultural Village, George Flores Old Store and History Center, Guam Zoo, Gun Beach, Latte of Freedom, Plaza de España, Puntan Dos Amantes, Ritidian Point, Saint Joseph Catholic Church, San Vitores Shrine, Tumon Beach, War in the Pacific National Historical Park, Ypao Beach

DATE VISITED:

WEATHER:

WHERE I WENT:

WHERE I STAYED:

WHO I WENT WITH:

FAVORITE MOMENT:

BEST DRIVING OR WALKING TOUR:

WHAT I'D RECOMMEND:

TIPS TO FRIENDS/FAMILY:

WHAT I WISH I KNEW BEFORE GOING:

WHAT WAS THE FIRST THING I NOTICED WHEN I ARRIVED?

MY FAVORITE PART OF THE VISIT WAS . . .

HOW I SPENT MY TIME THERE:

WHAT WOULD I DO IF I GO BACK?

WHAT IS SOMETHING I LEARNED THERE?

MY TOP THREE FAVORITE ACTIVITIES WERE . . .

1.

2.

3

MY TRIP WAS

/10

JAN   FEB   MAR   APR   MAY   JUN   JUL   AUG   SEP   OCT   NOV   DEC
1 2 3 4 5 6 7 8 9 10 11 12 13 14 15 16 17 18 19 20 21 22 23 24 25 26 27 28 29 30 31

Hawaii

STATE CAPITAL: Honolulu | **POPULATION:** 1,440,196 *(July 2022)*
STATE NICKNAME: The Aloha State | **YEAR OF STATEHOOD:** 1959
FUN FACT: Mauna Kea is the tallest mountain in the world, standing at
33,496 feet when measured from base (which is partially underwater) to peak.

MAIN ATTRACTIONS:

CITIES: Hana, Hilo, Honolulu, Pearl City, Pukalani, Waikiki

LANDSCAPES: Diamond Head State Monument, Haleakalā National Park, Hanalei Bay, Hoʻokipa Beach Park, Kealakekua Bay State Historical Park, Kīpahulu District, Kohala, Kona Coast, Mauna Kea, Mauna Loa, Nāpali Coast, Polihale State Park, Puʻuhonua o Hōnaunau National Historical Park, Waimea Canyon State Park, Waipiʻo Valley

POINTS OF INTEREST: Ahihi-Kinau Natural Area Reserve, Aliiolani Hale, Banyan Drive, Bishop Museum, Honolulu Museum of Art, Honolulu Zoo, ʻIolani Palace, Kalaupapa National Historical Park, Keomuku ghost town, Kualoa Ranch, Lānaʻi Culture & Heritage Center, Maui Ocean Center, Pacific Tsunami Museum, Palace Theater, Panaʻewa Rainforest Zoo & Gardens, Pearl Harbor National Memorial, Polynesian Cultural Center, Waikiki Aquarium

DATE VISITED:

WEATHER:

WHERE I WENT:

WHERE I STAYED:

WHO I WENT WITH:

FAVORITE MOMENT:

BEST DRIVING OR WALKING TOUR:

WHAT I'D RECOMMEND:

TIPS TO FRIENDS/FAMILY:

WHAT I WISH I KNEW BEFORE GOING:

WHAT WAS THE FIRST THING I NOTICED WHEN I ARRIVED?

MY FAVORITE PART OF THE VISIT WAS . . .

HOW I SPENT MY TIME THERE:

WHAT WOULD I DO IF I GO BACK?

WHAT IS SOMETHING I LEARNED THERE?

MY TOP THREE FAVORITE ACTIVITIES WERE . . .

1.

2.

3

MY TRIP WAS

JAN	FEB	MAR	APR	MAY	JUN	JUL	AUG	SEP	OCT	NOV	DEC
1 2 3	4 5 6	7 8 9	10 11 12	13 14 15	16 17	18 19 20	21 22	23 24 25	26 27	28 29	30 31

....

....

....

....

....

....

....

....

....

....

....

....

....

....

....

....

....

....

....

....

....

Idaho

STATE CAPITAL: Boise | **POPULATION:** 1,939,033 *(July 2022)*
STATE NICKNAME: The Gem State | **YEAR OF STATEHOOD:** 1890
FUN FACT: At 7,993 feet deep, Hells Canyon boasts the deepest river gorge in the U.S., exceeding the depth of the Grand Canyon.

MAIN ATTRACTIONS:

CITIES: Blackfoot, Boise, Coeur d'Alene, Fort Hall, Jerome, Ketchum, Lewiston, Mountain Home, Pocatello, Sun Valley, Twin Falls

LANDSCAPES: Bald Mountain, Bogus Basin, Boise River Greenbelt, Bruneau Dunes State Park, Craters of the Moon National Monument & Preserve, Dierkes Lake Park, Hells Canyon National Recreation Area, Lava Hot Springs, Nez Perce National Historical Park, Salmon River Mountains, Sawtooth National Recreation Area, Smoky Mountains, Shoshone Falls, Snake River Valley

POINTS OF INTEREST: Basque Museum & Cultural Center, Bruneau Dunes Observatory, Idaho Black History Museum, Idaho Botanical Garden, Idaho National Laboratory, Idaho Potato Museum, Minidoka National Historic Site, Pioneer Village, Julia Davis Park Rose Garden, Route of the Hiawatha, Silverwood Theme Park, World Center for Birds of Prey, Zoo Boise

DATE VISITED:

WEATHER:

WHERE I WENT:

WHERE I STAYED:

WHO I WENT WITH:

FAVORITE MOMENT:

BEST DRIVING OR WALKING TOUR:

WHAT I'D RECOMMEND:

TIPS TO FRIENDS/FAMILY:

WHAT I WISH I KNEW BEFORE GOING:

WHAT WAS THE FIRST THING I NOTICED WHEN I ARRIVED?

MY FAVORITE PART OF THE VISIT WAS . . .

HOW I SPENT MY TIME THERE:

WHAT WOULD I DO IF I GO BACK?

WHAT IS SOMETHING I LEARNED THERE?

MY TOP THREE FAVORITE ACTIVITIES WERE . . .

1.

2.

3

MY TRIP WAS

JAN   FEB   MAR   APR   MAY   JUN   JUL   AUG   SEP   OCT   NOV   DEC
1   2   3   4   5   6   7   8   9   10   11   12   13   14   15   16   17   18   19   20   21   22   23   24   25   26   27   28   29   30   31

....

....

....

....

....

....

....

....

....

....

....

....

....

....

....

....

....

....

....

....

....

....

....

Illinois

STATE CAPITAL: Springfield | **POPULATION:** 12,582,032 *(July 2022)*
STATE NICKNAME: The Prairie State | **YEAR OF STATEHOOD:** 1818
FUN FACT: The Nabisco factory in Chicago is the world's largest bakery, sitting at 1.8 million square feet.

MAIN ATTRACTIONS:

CITIES: Aurora, Collinsville, Chicago, Evanston, Galena, Metropolis, Naperville, Nauvoo, Oak Park, Quincy, Rockford, Springfield, Vandalia

LANDSCAPES: Fort Defiance State Park, Garden of the Gods Recreation Area, Mississippi River, Ohio River, Pounds Hollow Recreation Area, Rim Rock National Recreation Trail, Shawnee National Forest

POINTS OF INTEREST: Abraham Lincoln Presidential Library and Museum, Adler Planetarium, Anderson Japanese Gardens, Cahokia Mounds State Historic Site, "Cloud Gate," Chicago's Magnificent Mile, Chicago Water Tower, Ernest Hemingway Birthplace Museum, Kaskaskia Dragon, Klehm Arboretum & Botanic Garden, Lincoln Memorial Garden & Nature Center, Lincoln Park Zoo, Midway Village Museum, Millennium Park, Nicholas Conservatory & Gardens, Oak Ridge Cemetery, Prairie Avenue District, Shedd Aquarium, Super Museum, Willis Tower

DATE VISITED:

WEATHER:

WHERE I WENT:

WHERE I STAYED:

WHO I WENT WITH:

FAVORITE MOMENT:

BEST DRIVING OR WALKING TOUR:

WHAT I'D RECOMMEND:

TIPS TO FRIENDS/FAMILY:

WHAT I WISH I KNEW BEFORE GOING:

WHAT WAS THE FIRST THING I NOTICED WHEN I ARRIVED?

MY FAVORITE PART OF THE VISIT WAS . . .

HOW I SPENT MY TIME THERE:

WHAT WOULD I DO IF I GO BACK?

WHAT IS SOMETHING I LEARNED THERE?

MY TOP THREE FAVORITE ACTIVITIES WERE . . .

1.

2.

3

MY TRIP WAS

10

JAN		FEB			MAR			APR			MAY			JUN			JUL			AUG			SEP			OCT			NOV			DEC
1	2	3	4	5	6	7	8	9	10	11	12	13	14	15	16	17	18	19	20	21	22	23	24	25	26	27	28	29	30	31

Indiana

STATE CAPITAL: Indianapolis | **POPULATION:** 6,833,037 *(July 2022)*
STATE NICKNAME: The Hoosier State | **YEAR OF STATEHOOD:** 1816
FUN FACT: Indiana is dubbed the "Crossroads of America" due to the many major highways that traverse the state.

MAIN ATTRACTIONS:

CITIES: Bloomington, Evansville, Fishers, Fort Wayne, French Lick, Indianapolis, Marengo, Peru, Santa Claus, Shipshewana, South Bend, West Lafayette

LANDSCAPES: Brown County State Park, George Rogers Clark National Historical Park, Hoosier National Forest, Indiana Dunes National Park, Marengo Cave

POINTS OF INTEREST: Angel Mounds State Historic Site, Auburn Cord Duesenberg Automobile Museum, Blue Gate Theatre, Conner Prairie, DeBrand Fine Chocolates, Eiteljorg Museum of American Indians and Western Art, Holiday World & Splashin' Safari, Indianapolis Motor Speedway, Lockerbie Square Historic Neighborhood, Maple Grove Road, NCAA Hall of Champions, Pierogi Fest, U.S.S. *LST* Ship Memorial, White River Wapahani Trail

---

DATE VISITED:

WEATHER:

WHERE I WENT:

WHERE I STAYED:

WHO I WENT WITH:

FAVORITE MOMENT:

BEST DRIVING OR WALKING TOUR:

WHAT I'D RECOMMEND:

TIPS TO FRIENDS/FAMILY:

WHAT I WISH I KNEW BEFORE GOING:

WHAT WAS THE FIRST THING I NOTICED WHEN I ARRIVED?

MY FAVORITE PART OF THE VISIT WAS . . .

HOW I SPENT MY TIME THERE:

WHAT WOULD I DO IF I GO BACK?

WHAT IS SOMETHING I LEARNED THERE?

MY TOP THREE FAVORITE ACTIVITIES WERE . . .

1.

2.

3

MY TRIP WAS

/10

JAN   FEB   MAR   APR   MAY   JUN   JUL   AUG   SEP   OCT   NOV   DEC

1 2 3 4 5 6 7 8 9 10 11 12 13 14 15 16 17 18 19 20 21 22 23 24 25 26 27 28 29 30 31

Iowa

STATE CAPITAL: Des Moines | **POPULATION:** 3,200,517 *(July 2022)*
STATE NICKNAME: The Hawkeye State | **YEAR OF STATEHOOD:** 1846
FUN FACT: Dubuque's 1893 Fenelon Place Elevator, a narrow-gauge funicular, claims to be the world's steepest and shortest railroad line.

MAIN ATTRACTIONS:

CITIES: Altoona, Boone, Cedar Rapids, Davenport, Des Moines, Dubuque, Dundee, Dyersville, Hamburg, Iowa City, Marquette, Sioux City, Waterloo, West Branch

LANDSCAPES: Backbone Lake, Backbone State Park, Des Moines River Valley, Ledges State Park, Loess Hills State Forest, Maquoketa Caves State Park, Pikes Peak State Park, Waubonsie State Park

POINTS OF INTEREST: Adventureland Resort, Amana Colonies, Dubuque Arboretum & Botanical Gardens, *Field of Dreams* Movie Site, Figge Art Museum, Herbert Hoover National Historic Site, Iowa State Fair, National Czech & Slovak Museum & Library, National Mississippi River Museum & Aquarium, Palmer's Olde Tyme Candy Shoppe, Salisbury House & Gardens, Science Center of Iowa, Sioux City Lewis & Clark Interpretive Center, Trinity Heights, Western Gateway Park, World Food Prize Hall of Laureates

DATE VISITED:

WEATHER:

WHERE I WENT:

WHERE I STAYED:

WHO I WENT WITH:

FAVORITE MOMENT:

BEST DRIVING OR WALKING TOUR:

WHAT I'D RECOMMEND:

TIPS TO FRIENDS/FAMILY:

WHAT I WISH I KNEW BEFORE GOING:

WHAT WAS THE FIRST THING I NOTICED WHEN I ARRIVED?

MY FAVORITE PART OF THE VISIT WAS . . .

HOW I SPENT MY TIME THERE:

WHAT WOULD I DO IF I GO BACK?

WHAT IS SOMETHING I LEARNED THERE?

MY TOP THREE FAVORITE ACTIVITIES WERE . . .

1.

2.

3

MY TRIP WAS

/10

JAN   FEB   MAR   APR   MAY   JUN   JUL   AUG   SEP   OCT   NOV   DEC
1   2   3   4   5   6   7   8   9   10   11   12   13   14   15   16   17   18   19   20   21   22   23   24   25   26   27   28   29   30   31

Kansas

STATE CAPITAL: Topeka | **POPULATION:** 2,937,150 *(July 2022)*
STATE NICKNAME: The Sunflower State | **YEAR OF STATEHOOD:** 1861
FUN FACT: Fort Scott National Cemetery, which is two years older than Arlington National Cemetery, was the nation's first.

MAIN ATTRACTIONS:

CITIES: Abilene, Atchison, Dodge City, Galena, Hutchinson, Larned, Lawrence, Lucas, Overland Park, Topeka, Wichita

LANDSCAPES: Flint Hills, Tallgrass Prairie National Preserve

POINTS OF INTEREST: Amelia Earhart Birthplace Museum, Boot Hill Museum, Botanica, *Brown v. Board of Education* National Historic Site, Cosmosphere, Dickinson County Heritage Center and Museum, Eisenhower Presidential Library, Museum & Boyhood Home, Fort Scott National Historic Site, Kansas Aviation Museum, Kansas Wildlife Exhibit, "Keeper of the Plains" sculpture, Mid-America All-Indian Center, Old Cowtown Museum, Old Prairie Town/Ward-Meade Historic Site, Overland Park Arboretum & Botanical Gardens, Science City, Sedgwick County Zoo, S. P. Dinsmoor's Garden of Eden, Strataca

DATE VISITED:	WHO I WENT WITH:	WHAT I'D RECOMMEND:
WEATHER:		
	FAVORITE MOMENT:	**TIPS TO FRIENDS/FAMILY:**
WHERE I WENT:		
	BEST DRIVING OR WALKING TOUR:	**WHAT I WISH I KNEW BEFORE GOING:**
WHERE I STAYED:		

WHAT WAS THE FIRST THING I NOTICED WHEN I ARRIVED?

MY FAVORITE PART OF THE VISIT WAS . . .

HOW I SPENT MY TIME THERE:

WHAT WOULD I DO IF I GO BACK?

WHAT IS SOMETHING I LEARNED THERE?

MY TOP THREE FAVORITE ACTIVITIES WERE . . .

1.

2.

3

MY TRIP WAS

/10

JAN   FEB   MAR   APR   MAY   JUN   JUL   AUG   SEP   OCT   NOV   DEC

1   2   3   4   5   6   7   8   9   10   11   12   13   14   15   16   17   18   19   20   21   22   23   24   25   26   27   28   29   30   31

Kentucky

STATE CAPITAL: Frankfort | **POPULATION:** 4,512,310 *(July 2022)*
STATE NICKNAME: The Bluegrass State | **YEAR OF STATEHOOD:** 1792
FUN FACT: Under a full moon and clear night sky, visitors can see a "moonbow" (lunar rainbow) at the base of Cumberland Falls.

MAIN ATTRACTIONS:

CITIES: Bardstown, Bowling Green, Clermont, Corbin, Danville, Fort Knox, Frankfort, Harlan, Lawrenceburg, Lexington, London, Louisville, Pikeville, Versailles

LANDSCAPES: Big South Fork National River & Recreation Area, Cumberland Falls State Resort Park, Cumberland Gap, Cumberland Mountains, Daniel Boone National Forest, Diamond Caverns, Frozen Niagara, Louisville Mega Cavern, Mammoth Cave National Park

POINTS OF INTEREST: Cave Hill Cemetery, Churchill Downs, Conrad-Caldwell House Museum, Evan Williams Bourbon Experience, Frazier History Museum, Kentucky Bourbon Trail, Kentucky Horse Park, Locust Grove, Louisville Slugger Museum & Factory, Mary Todd Lincoln House, Muhammad Ali Center, Newport Aquarium, Oscar Getz Museum of Whiskey History, Shaker Village of Pleasant Hill, Waterfront Park, Woodford Reserve Distillery

DATE VISITED:

WEATHER:

WHERE I WENT:

WHERE I STAYED:

WHO I WENT WITH:

FAVORITE MOMENT:

BEST DRIVING OR WALKING TOUR:

WHAT I'D RECOMMEND:

TIPS TO FRIENDS/FAMILY:

WHAT I WISH I KNEW BEFORE GOING:

WHAT WAS THE FIRST THING I NOTICED WHEN I ARRIVED?

MY FAVORITE PART OF THE VISIT WAS . . .

HOW I SPENT MY TIME THERE:

WHAT WOULD I DO IF I GO BACK?

WHAT IS SOMETHING I LEARNED THERE?

MY TOP THREE FAVORITE ACTIVITIES WERE . . .

1.

2.

3

MY TRIP WAS

/10

JAN   FEB   MAR   APR   MAY   JUN   JUL   AUG   SEP   OCT   NOV   DEC

1 2 3 4 5 6 7 8 9 10 11 12 13 14 15 16 17 18 19 20 21 22 23 24 25 26 27 28 29 30 31

Louisiana

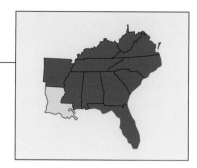

STATE CAPITAL: Baton Rouge | **POPULATION:** 4,590,241 *(July 2022)*
STATE NICKNAME: The Pelican State | **YEAR OF STATEHOOD:** 1812
FUN FACT: Louisiana's art deco capitol building is the tallest state capitol in the nation, standing at 34 stories and 450 feet.

MAIN ATTRACTIONS:

CITIES: Alexandria, Baton Rouge, Breaux Bridge, Ferriday, Grand Isle, Lafayette, Lake Charles, Natchitoches, New Orleans, St. Francisville, Thibodaux

LANDSCAPES: Barataria Preserve, Bayou Country, Cane River National Heritage Area, Cypremort Point State Park, Gulf of Mexico, Jean Lafitte National Historical Park and Preserve, Lake Bistineau State Park, Mississippi River, Red River

POINTS OF INTEREST: Acadiana Symphony Orchestra & Conservatory of Music, Black Heritage Gallery, Destrehan Plantation, French Quarter, Garden District, Great River Road, Louisiana Art & Science Museum, Louisiana State Capitol, Louisiana's Old State Capitol, Louisiana Prison Museum & Cultural Center, Mardi Gras World, Metairie Cemetery, National WWII Museum, New Orleans City Park, Pere Antoine Alley, the Presbytère, St. Louis Cathedral, Vermilionville, Wetlands Acadian Cultural Center

DATE VISITED:

WEATHER:

WHERE I WENT:

WHERE I STAYED:

WHO I WENT WITH:

FAVORITE MOMENT:

BEST DRIVING OR WALKING TOUR:

WHAT I'D RECOMMEND:

TIPS TO FRIENDS/FAMILY:

WHAT I WISH I KNEW BEFORE GOING:

WHAT WAS THE FIRST THING I NOTICED WHEN I ARRIVED?

MY FAVORITE PART OF THE VISIT WAS . . .

HOW I SPENT MY TIME THERE:

WHAT WOULD I DO IF I GO BACK?

WHAT IS SOMETHING I LEARNED THERE?

MY TOP THREE FAVORITE ACTIVITIES WERE . . .

1.

2.

3

MY TRIP WAS

/10

JAN	FEB	MAR	APR	MAY	JUN	JUL	AUG	SEP	OCT	NOV	DEC
1 2 3	4 5 6	7 8 9	10 11 12	13 14 15	16 17	18 19 20	21 22	23 24	25 26 27	28 29	30 31

Maine

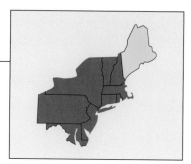

STATE CAPITAL: Augusta | **POPULATION:** 1,385,340 *(July 2022)*
STATE NICKNAME: The Pine Tree State | **YEAR OF STATEHOOD:** 1820
FUN FACT: Old Fort Western in Augusta was originally built in 1754 and is the oldest surviving wooden fort in New England.

MAIN ATTRACTIONS:

CITIES: Augusta, Bar Harbor, Blue Hill, Boothbay Harbor, Brunswick, Cape Elizabeth, Kennebunkport, Ogunquit, Portland, Trenton

LANDSCAPES: Acadia National Park, Allagash Wilderness Waterway, Baxter State Park, Camden Hills State Park, Casco Bay, Churchill Lake, Fore River, Fort Williams Park, Monhegan Island, Mount Battie, Mount Desert Island, Mount Katahdin, North Maine Woods, Ogunquit Beach, Penobscot Bay, White Mountains

POINTS OF INTEREST: Boothbay Railway Village, Coastal Maine Botanical Gardens, Goddard Mansion, Maine Narrow Gauge Railroad Co. & Museum, Maine State Museum, Marginal Way, McLellan-Sweat Mansion, Oceanarium and Education Center, Old Fort Western, Old Port district, Portland Head Light, Portland Museum of Art, Portland Observatory, Seashore Trolley Museum, Sugarloaf winter resort, Timber Tina's Great Maine Lumberjack Show, Victoria Mansion, Wadsworth-Longfellow House

DATE VISITED:

WEATHER:

WHERE I WENT:

WHERE I STAYED:

WHO I WENT WITH:

FAVORITE MOMENT:

BEST DRIVING OR WALKING TOUR:

WHAT I'D RECOMMEND:

TIPS TO FRIENDS/FAMILY:

WHAT I WISH I KNEW BEFORE GOING:

WHAT WAS THE FIRST THING I NOTICED WHEN I ARRIVED?

MY FAVORITE PART OF THE VISIT WAS . . .

HOW I SPENT MY TIME THERE:

WHAT WOULD I DO IF I GO BACK?

WHAT IS SOMETHING I LEARNED THERE?

MY TOP THREE FAVORITE ACTIVITIES WERE . . .

1.

2.

3

MY TRIP WAS

/10

JAN   FEB   MAR   APR   MAY   JUN   JUL   AUG   SEP   OCT   NOV   DEC
1   2   3   4   5   6   7   8   9   10   11   12   13   14   15   16   17   18   19   20   21   22   23   24   25   26   27   28   29   30   31

Maryland

STATE CAPITAL: Annapolis | **POPULATION:** 6,164,660 *(July 2022)*
STATE NICKNAME: The Old Line State | **YEAR OF STATEHOOD:** 1788
FUN FACT: The Chesapeake Bay is where more than 150 freshwater rivers and streams meet the Atlantic.

MAIN ATTRACTIONS:

CITIES: Annapolis, Baltimore, Cumberland, Frederick, Greenbelt, Ocean City

LANDSCAPES: Allegheny Mountains, Assateague Island National Seashore, Catoctin Mountain Park, Chesapeake Bay, Deep Creek Lake, Locust Point, Patapsco River, Savage River State Forest

POINTS OF INTEREST: American Visionary Art Museum, Baltimore Museum of Industry, Carroll County Farm Museum, Fell's Point, Hammond-Harwood House, Inner Harbor of Baltimore, Kunta Kinte–Alex Haley Memorial, Maryland Science Center, Maryland State House, Monocacy National Battlefield, Mount Vernon Cultural District, NASA Goddard Space Flight Center, National Aquarium, National Museum of Civil War Medicine, Pier Six Pavilion, U.S. Naval Academy, U.S.S. *Constellation,* Walters Art Museum, William Paca House & Garden

DATE VISITED:

WEATHER:

WHERE I WENT:

WHERE I STAYED:

WHO I WENT WITH:

FAVORITE MOMENT:

BEST DRIVING OR WALKING TOUR:

WHAT I'D RECOMMEND:

TIPS TO FRIENDS/FAMILY:

WHAT I WISH I KNEW BEFORE GOING:

WHAT WAS THE FIRST THING I NOTICED WHEN I ARRIVED?

MY FAVORITE PART OF THE VISIT WAS . . .

HOW I SPENT MY TIME THERE:

WHAT WOULD I DO IF I GO BACK?

WHAT IS SOMETHING I LEARNED THERE?

MY TOP THREE FAVORITE ACTIVITIES WERE . . .

1.

2.

3

MY TRIP WAS

10

JAN	FEB	MAR	APR	MAY	JUN	JUL	AUG	SEP	OCT	NOV	DEC
1 2 3	4 5 6	7 8 9	10 11 12	13 14 15	16 17	18 19 20	21 22	23 24 25	26 27	28 29 30	31

Massachusetts

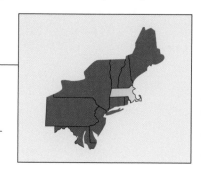

STATE CAPITAL: Boston | **POPULATION:** 6,981,974 *(July 2022)*
STATE NICKNAME: The Bay State | **YEAR OF STATEHOOD:** 1788
FUN FACT: The game of basketball was invented in Springfield, Massachusetts, in 1891.

MAIN ATTRACTIONS:

CITIES: Barnstable, Boston, Cambridge, Chatham, Gloucester, Lexington, Nantucket, New Bedford, Newton, Northampton, Pittsfield, Plymouth, Provincetown, Quincy, Salem, Springfield, Truro, Worcester

LANDSCAPES: The Berkshires, Boston Harbor Islands National Recreation Area, Cape Cod National Seashore, Minute Man National Historical Park

POINTS OF INTEREST: Adams National Historical Park, Beacon Hill, Boston African American National Historic Site, Boston Tea Party Ships & Museum, Bunker Hill Monument, Charlestown Navy Yard, Copp's Hill Burying Ground, Dr. Seuss National Memorial Sculpture Garden, Fenway Park, Harvard University, John F. Kennedy Presidential Library and Museum, Museum of Fine Arts Boston, New Bedford Whaling Museum, New England Aquarium, Old Sturbridge Village, Paul Revere House, Pilgrim Hall Museum, Plymouth Rock, Rotch-Jones-Duff House & Garden Museum, Witch Dungeon Museum

DATE VISITED:

WEATHER:

WHERE I WENT:

WHERE I STAYED:

WHO I WENT WITH:

FAVORITE MOMENT:

BEST DRIVING OR WALKING TOUR:

WHAT I'D RECOMMEND:

TIPS TO FRIENDS/FAMILY:

WHAT I WISH I KNEW BEFORE GOING:

WHAT WAS THE FIRST THING I NOTICED WHEN I ARRIVED?

MY FAVORITE PART OF THE VISIT WAS . . .

HOW I SPENT MY TIME THERE:

WHAT WOULD I DO IF I GO BACK?

WHAT IS SOMETHING I LEARNED THERE?

MY TOP THREE FAVORITE ACTIVITIES WERE . . .

1.

2.

3

MY TRIP WAS

/10

JAN   FEB   MAR   APR   MAY   JUN   JUL   AUG   SEP   OCT   NOV   DEC

1 2 3 4 5 6 7 8 9 10 11 12 13 14 15 16 17 18 19 20 21 22 23 24 25 26 27 28 29 30 31

Michigan

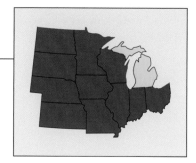

STATE CAPITAL: Lansing | **POPULATION:** 10,034,113 *(July 2022)*
STATE NICKNAME: The Wolverine State | **YEAR OF STATEHOOD:** 1837
FUN FACT: Montague, Michigan, boasts the world's biggest weather vane, standing at 48 feet tall and weighing 4,300 pounds.

MAIN ATTRACTIONS:

CITIES: Ann Arbor, Copper Harbor, Dearborn, Detroit, Grand Rapids, Holland, Kalamazoo, Lansing, Leland, New Buffalo, Petoskey, Sault Ste. Marie, Traverse City

LANDSCAPES: Gold Coast, Grand Island National Recreation Area, Grand River, Grand Sable Banks, Hiawatha National Forest, Huron-Manistee National Forests, Isle Royale National Park, Mackinac Island State Park, Ottawa National Forest, Pictured Rocks National Lakeshore, Sleeping Bear Dunes National Lakeshore, Twelvemile Beach, Windmill Island Gardens

POINTS OF INTEREST: Charles H. Wright Museum of African American History, Colonial Michilimackinac, Detroit Riverfront, Detroit Zoo, Frederik Meijer Gardens & Sculpture Park, Gerald R. Ford Presidential Library & Museum, Henry Ford Museum of American Innovation, Mackinac Bridge, Matthaei Botanical Gardens, Michigan Science Center, Motown Museum, Museum Ship *Valley Camp,* Old Mission Peninsula

DATE VISITED:

WEATHER:

WHERE I WENT:

WHERE I STAYED:

WHO I WENT WITH:

FAVORITE MOMENT:

BEST DRIVING OR WALKING TOUR:

WHAT I'D RECOMMEND:

TIPS TO FRIENDS/FAMILY:

WHAT I WISH I KNEW BEFORE GOING:

WHAT WAS THE FIRST THING I NOTICED WHEN I ARRIVED?

MY FAVORITE PART OF THE VISIT WAS . . .

HOW I SPENT MY TIME THERE:

WHAT WOULD I DO IF I GO BACK?

WHAT IS SOMETHING I LEARNED THERE?

MY TOP THREE FAVORITE ACTIVITIES WERE . . .

1.

2.

3

MY TRIP WAS

/10

JAN   FEB   MAR   APR   MAY   JUN   JUL   AUG   SEP   OCT   NOV   DEC

1 2 3 4 5 6 7 8 9 10 11 12 13 14 15 16 17 18 19 20 21 22 23 24 25 26 27 28 29 30 31

Minnesota

STATE CAPITAL: St. Paul | **POPULATION:** 5,717,184 *(July 2022)*
STATE NICKNAME: The North Star State | **YEAR OF STATEHOOD:** 1858
FUN FACT: St. Anthony Falls, located at the northeast edge of Minneapolis, is the only natural waterfall on the Mississippi River.

MAIN ATTRACTIONS:

CITIES: Brainerd, Duluth, Ely, Hibbing, Minneapolis, St. Cloud, St. Paul, Stillwater, Wabasha, Winona

LANDSCAPES: Boundary Waters Canoe Area Wilderness, Grand Portage State Park, Hollow Rock, Kabetogama Peninsula, Mesabi Iron Range, Mesabi Trail, Minnehaha Regional Park, Park Point Recreation Area, Pipestone National Monument, St. Anthony Falls, St. Croix National Scenic Riverway, Voyageurs National Park

POINTS OF INTEREST: Cathedral of St. Paul, Duluth's Rose Garden, Fort Snelling, Guthrie Theater, International Wolf Center, James J. Hill House, Landmark Center, Mall of America, Minneapolis Sculpture Garden, Minnesota Children's Museum, Minnesota Slip Bridge, Munsinger Clemens Gardens, National Eagle Center, Ordway Center for the Performing Arts, Paul Bunyan Land, Science Museum of Minnesota, Stone Arch Bridge, Walker Art Center, Weisman Art Museum, Witch Tree

DATE VISITED:

WEATHER:

WHERE I WENT:

WHERE I STAYED:

WHO I WENT WITH:

FAVORITE MOMENT:

BEST DRIVING OR WALKING TOUR:

WHAT I'D RECOMMEND:

TIPS TO FRIENDS/FAMILY:

WHAT I WISH I KNEW BEFORE GOING:

WHAT WAS THE FIRST THING I NOTICED WHEN I ARRIVED?

MY FAVORITE PART OF THE VISIT WAS . . .

HOW I SPENT MY TIME THERE:

WHAT WOULD I DO IF I GO BACK?

WHAT IS SOMETHING I LEARNED THERE?

MY TOP THREE FAVORITE ACTIVITIES WERE . . .

1.

2.

3

MY TRIP WAS

10

JAN   FEB   MAR   APR   MAY   JUN   JUL   AUG   SEP   OCT   NOV   DEC
1 2 3 4 5 6 7 8 9 10 11 12 13 14 15 16 17 18 19 20 21 22 23 24 25 26 27 28 29 30 31

Mississippi

STATE CAPITAL: Jackson | **POPULATION:** 2,940,057 *(July 2022)*
STATE NICKNAME: The Magnolia State | **YEAR OF STATEHOOD:** 1817
FUN FACT: Dockery Farms, a 25,600-acre former cotton plantation and sawmill, is widely regarded as the place where Delta blues music was born.

MAIN ATTRACTIONS:

CITIES: Biloxi, Clarksdale, Fondren, Gulfport, Jackson, Ocean Springs, Oxford, Tupelo, Vicksburg

LANDSCAPES: Cat Island, Gulf Islands National Seashore, LeFleur's Bluff State Park, Natchez Trace Parkway, Tishomingo State Park, West Ship Island

POINTS OF INTEREST: Delta Blues Museum, Dockery Farms, Dunleith Historic Inn, Lynn Meadows Discovery Center, Malaco Records, Medgar Evers Home Museum, Mississippi Children's Museum, Mississippi Governor's Mansion, Mississippi Museum of Art, Natchez National Historical Park, Natchez Pilgrimage Tours, Old Depot Museum, Rowan Oak, Tupelo National Battlefield, U.S. Army Corps of Engineers Lower Mississippi River Museum & Riverfront Interpretive Site, Vicksburg National Military Park, Walter Anderson Museum of Art, Walton-Young Historic House

DATE VISITED:

WEATHER:

WHERE I WENT:

WHERE I STAYED:

WHO I WENT WITH:

FAVORITE MOMENT:

BEST DRIVING OR WALKING TOUR:

WHAT I'D RECOMMEND:

TIPS TO FRIENDS/FAMILY:

WHAT I WISH I KNEW BEFORE GOING:

WHAT WAS THE FIRST THING I NOTICED WHEN I ARRIVED?

MY FAVORITE PART OF THE VISIT WAS . . .

HOW I SPENT MY TIME THERE:

WHAT WOULD I DO IF I GO BACK?

WHAT IS SOMETHING I LEARNED THERE?

MY TOP THREE FAVORITE ACTIVITIES WERE . . .

1.

2.

3

MY TRIP WAS

10

JAN   FEB   MAR   APR   MAY   JUN   JUL   AUG   SEP   OCT   NOV   DEC
1 2 3 4 5 6 7 8 9 10 11 12 13 14 15 16 17 18 19 20 21 22 23 24 25 26 27 28 29 30 31

Missouri

STATE CAPITAL: Jefferson City | **POPULATION:** 6,177,957 *(July 2022)*
STATE NICKNAME: The Show-Me State | **YEAR OF STATEHOOD:** 1821
FUN FACT: The Gateway Arch, located in St. Louis, is as wide as it is tall.

MAIN ATTRACTIONS:

CITIES: Branson, Hannibal, Independence, Jefferson City, Kansas City, St. Joseph, St. Louis, Springfield

LANDSCAPES: Castlewood State Park, Elephant Rocks State Park, Forest Park, Lake of the Ozarks, Nathanael Greene/Close Memorial Park, Ozark National Scenic Riverways

POINTS OF INTEREST: *Arabia* Steamboat Museum, Busch Stadium, Gateway Arch, Hallmark Kaleidoscope, Harry S. Truman National Historic Site, Jefferson Landing State Historic Site, Kemper Museum of Contemporary Art, Johnny Morris Wonders of Wildlife National Museum & Aquarium, Laclede's Landing, Liberty Memorial Tower, Mark Twain Boyhood Home & Museum, Missouri Botanical Garden, Missouri History Museum, National World War I Museum and Memorial, Nelson-Atkins Museum of Art, Saint Louis Art Museum, Saint Louis Zoo, Science City, Silver Dollar City, Wilson's Creek National Battlefield

DATE VISITED:

WEATHER:

WHERE I WENT:

WHERE I STAYED:

WHO I WENT WITH:

FAVORITE MOMENT:

BEST DRIVING OR WALKING TOUR:

WHAT I'D RECOMMEND:

TIPS TO FRIENDS/FAMILY:

WHAT I WISH I KNEW BEFORE GOING:

WHAT WAS THE FIRST THING I NOTICED WHEN I ARRIVED?

MY FAVORITE PART OF THE VISIT WAS . . .

HOW I SPENT MY TIME THERE:

WHAT WOULD I DO IF I GO BACK?

WHAT IS SOMETHING I LEARNED THERE?

MY TOP THREE FAVORITE ACTIVITIES WERE . . .

1.

2.

3

MY TRIP WAS

10

JAN   FEB   MAR   APR   MAY   JUN   JUL   AUG   SEP   OCT   NOV   DEC
1 2 3 4 5 6 7 8 9 10 11 12 13 14 15 16 17 18 19 20 21 22 23 24 25 26 27 28 29 30 31

Montana

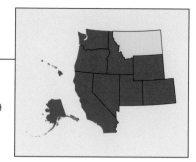

STATE CAPITAL: Helena | **POPULATION:** 1,122,867 *(July 2022)*
STATE NICKNAME: The Treasure State | **YEAR OF STATEHOOD:** 1889
FUN FACT: Montana has the largest glacier gathering in the lower 48.

MAIN ATTRACTIONS:

CITIES: Bannack, Billings, Bozeman, Butte, Gardiner, Great Falls, Helena, Livingston, Missoula, Polson, Virginia City, West Yellowstone, Whitefish

LANDSCAPES: Bighorn Canyon National Recreation Area, Crow Reservation, Fort Peck Lake, Glacier National Park, Logan Pass, St. Mary Lake, Upper Missouri River Breaks National Monument, Yellowstone National Park

POINTS OF INTEREST: Berkeley Pit, Big Sky Resort, Bridger Bowl, Butte-Anaconda Historic District, A Carousel for Missoula, Cathedral of Saint Helena, C.M. Russell Museum, Going-to-the-Sun Road, Grant-Kohrs Ranch National Historic Site, Grinnell Glacier, Grizzly & Wolf Discovery Center, Iceberg Lake, Montana's Museum, Museum of the Rockies, Smokejumper Visitor Center, Western Heritage Center, Whitefish Mountain Resort, World Museum of Mining, Yellowstone Art Museum

DATE VISITED:

WEATHER:

WHERE I WENT:

WHERE I STAYED:

WHO I WENT WITH:

FAVORITE MOMENT:

BEST DRIVING OR WALKING TOUR:

WHAT I'D RECOMMEND:

TIPS TO FRIENDS/FAMILY:

WHAT I WISH I KNEW BEFORE GOING:

WHAT WAS THE FIRST THING I NOTICED WHEN I ARRIVED?

MY FAVORITE PART OF THE VISIT WAS . . .

HOW I SPENT MY TIME THERE:

WHAT WOULD I DO IF I GO BACK?

WHAT IS SOMETHING I LEARNED THERE?

MY TOP THREE FAVORITE ACTIVITIES WERE . . .

1.

2.

3

MY TRIP WAS

/10

119

JAN   FEB   MAR   APR   MAY   JUN   JUL   AUG   SEP   OCT   NOV   DEC
1 2 3 4 5 6 7 8 9 10 11 12 13 14 15 16 17 18 19 20 21 22 23 24 25 26 27 28 29 30 31

Nebraska

STATE CAPITAL: Lincoln | **POPULATION:** 1,967,923 *(July 2022)*
STATE NICKNAME: The Cornhusker State | **YEAR OF STATEHOOD:** 1867
FUN FACT: More than nine million acres of Nebraska are planted with corn, nearly twice the acreage of the next largest crop.

MAIN ATTRACTIONS:

CITIES: Bellevue, Chadron, Crane Meadows, Gibbon, Kearney, Lexington, Lincoln, Minden, North Platte, Omaha, Roca

LANDSCAPES: Buffalo Bill Ranch State Historical Park, Homestead National Historical Park, Indian Cave State Park, Lewis & Clark National Historic Trail, Missouri National Recreational River, Nebraska National Forest, Nebraska Sandhills, Niobrara National Scenic River, Pioneers Park Nature Center, Platte River, Ponca State Park, Scotts Bluff National Monument, Valentine National Wildlife Refuge

POINTS OF INTEREST: Bob Kerrey Pedestrian Bridge, Carhenge, The Durham Museum, Gothenburg Pony Express Station, Heartland Museum of Military Vehicles, Heartland of America Park & Fountain, Joslyn Castle & Gardens, Lauritzen Gardens, Marx Science Discovery Center, Omaha Children's Museum, Omaha's Henry Doorly Zoo & Aquarium, Pioneer Village, Sheldon Museum of Art

DATE VISITED:	WHO I WENT WITH:	WHAT I'D RECOMMEND:
WEATHER:	FAVORITE MOMENT:	TIPS TO FRIENDS/FAMILY:
WHERE I WENT:		
WHERE I STAYED:	BEST DRIVING OR WALKING TOUR:	WHAT I WISH I KNEW BEFORE GOING:

WHAT WAS THE FIRST THING I NOTICED WHEN I ARRIVED?

MY FAVORITE PART OF THE VISIT WAS . . .

HOW I SPENT MY TIME THERE:

WHAT WOULD I DO IF I GO BACK?

WHAT IS SOMETHING I LEARNED THERE?

MY TOP THREE FAVORITE ACTIVITIES WERE . . .

1.

2.

3

MY TRIP WAS

10

JAN			FEB			MAR			APR			MAY			JUN			JUL			AUG			SEP			OCT			NOV			DEC
1	2	3	4	5	6	7	8	9	10	11	12	13	14	15	16	17	18	19	20	21	22	23	24	25	26	27	28	29	30	31

Nevada

STATE CAPITAL: Carson City | **POPULATION:** 3,177,772 *(July 2022)*
STATE NICKNAME: The Silver State | **YEAR OF STATEHOOD:** 1864
FUN FACT: Due to numerous claims of people seeing extraterrestrials along a stretch of State Route 375, the Nevada transportation board named it Extraterrestrial Highway in 1996.

MAIN ATTRACTIONS:

CITIES: Carson City, Elko, Las Vegas, Laughlin, Reno, Sparks, Virginia City

LANDSCAPES: Black Canyon National Water Trail, Black Rock Desert, Colorado River, Great Basin National Park, Kit Carson Trail, Lake Mead National Recreation Area, Lake Tahoe, Mojave Desert, Pyramid Lake, Sierra Nevada mountains, Red Rock Canyon National Conservation Area, Ruby Mountains, Valley of Fire State Park

POINTS OF INTEREST: Area 51, Bucket of Blood Saloon, Brewery Arts Center, Gold Point Ghost Town, Hoover Dam, Incline Village, Las Vegas Strip, Mandalay Bay's Shark Reef Aquarium, The Mob Museum, National Automobile Museum, National Cowboy Poetry Gathering, The Neon Museum, Nevada Museum of Art, Nevada State Railroad Museum, Fremont Street Experience, Reno Air Races, Rhyolite Ghost Town

---

DATE VISITED:

WEATHER:

WHERE I WENT:

WHERE I STAYED:

WHO I WENT WITH:

FAVORITE MOMENT:

BEST DRIVING OR WALKING TOUR:

WHAT I'D RECOMMEND:

TIPS TO FRIENDS/FAMILY:

WHAT I WISH I KNEW BEFORE GOING:

WHAT WAS THE FIRST THING I NOTICED WHEN I ARRIVED?

MY FAVORITE PART OF THE VISIT WAS . . .

HOW I SPENT MY TIME THERE:

WHAT WOULD I DO IF I GO BACK?

WHAT IS SOMETHING I LEARNED THERE?

MY TOP THREE FAVORITE ACTIVITIES WERE . . .

1.

2.

3

MY TRIP WAS

/10

JAN   FEB   MAR   APR   MAY   JUN   JUL   AUG   SEP   OCT   NOV   DEC

1 2 3 4 5 6 7 8 9 10 11 12 13 14 15 16 17 18 19 20 21 22 23 24 25 26 27 28 29 30 31

New Hampshire

STATE CAPITAL: Concord | **POPULATION:** 1,395,231 *(July 2022)*
STATE NICKNAME: The Granite State | **YEAR OF STATEHOOD:** 1788
FUN FACT: New Hampshire may be the only state with an official historical plaque marking an alien abduction, a 1961 incident on Route 3.

MAIN ATTRACTIONS:

CITIES: Concord, Conway, Franconia, Holderness, Jefferson, Lincoln, Manchester, Moultonborough, North Conway, Portsmouth, Rumney, Tamworth, Wolfeboro, Woodstock

LANDSCAPES: Amoskeag Falls, Isles of Shoals, Lake Massabesic, Lake Winnipesaukee, Merrimack River, Mount Monadnock State Park, Mount Washington State Park, Polar Caves Park, Presidential Range of the White Mountains, White Mountain National Forest

POINTS OF INTEREST: Castle in the Clouds, Conway Scenic Railroad, Currier Museum of Art, The Frost Place, Kimball Castle, McAuliffe-Shepard Discovery Center, Mount Washington Cog Railway, Mount Washington Observatory & Weather Discovery Center, New Hampshire Boat Museum, New Hampshire State House, the Palace Theatre, Portsmouth Athenaeum, Remick Country Doctor Museum & Farm, Saint-Gaudens National Historical Park, Strawbery Banke Museum

DATE VISITED:

WEATHER:

WHERE I WENT:

WHERE I STAYED:

WHO I WENT WITH:

FAVORITE MOMENT:

BEST DRIVING OR WALKING TOUR:

WHAT I'D RECOMMEND:

TIPS TO FRIENDS/FAMILY:

WHAT I WISH I KNEW BEFORE GOING:

WHAT WAS THE FIRST THING I NOTICED WHEN I ARRIVED?

MY FAVORITE PART OF THE VISIT WAS . . .

HOW I SPENT MY TIME THERE:

WHAT WOULD I DO IF I GO BACK?

WHAT IS SOMETHING I LEARNED THERE?

MY TOP THREE FAVORITE ACTIVITIES WERE . . .

1.

2.

3

MY TRIP WAS

JAN   FEB   MAR   APR   MAY   JUN   JUL   AUG   SEP   OCT   NOV   DEC

1   2   3   4   5   6   7   8   9   10   11   12   13   14   15   16   17   18   19   20   21   22   23   24   25   26   27   28   29   30   31

New Jersey

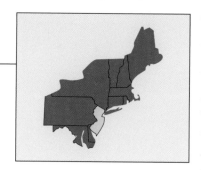

STATE CAPITAL: Trenton | **POPULATION:** 9,261,699 *(July 2022)*
STATE NICKNAME: The Garden State | **YEAR OF STATEHOOD:** 1787
FUN FACT: Albert Einstein carried out his final research at the Institute for Advanced Study on the Princeton University campus.

MAIN ATTRACTIONS:

CITIES: Atlantic City, Camden, Cape May, Elizabeth, Hamilton Township, Hoboken, Jersey City, Morristown, Newark, Passaic, Paterson, Princeton, Trenton, West Orange

LANDSCAPES: Delaware Water Gap National Recreation Area, Edwin B. Forsythe National Wildlife Refuge, Gateway National Recreation Area, Island Beach State Park, Liberty State Park, Paterson Great Falls National Historical Park, New Jersey Pinelands National Reserve, Washington Crossing State Park

POINTS OF INTEREST: Atlantic City Boardwalk, Battleship New Jersey, Cape May County Park & Zoo, Cathedral Basilica of the Sacred Heart, Central Railroad of New Jersey Terminal, Ellis Island National Immigration Museum, Grounds for Sculpture, Jersey Shore, Liberty Science Center, Long Beach Island, Navy Lakehurst Historical Society, Princeton University, Silverball Museum Arcade, Steel Pier, Thomas Edison National Historical Park

DATE VISITED:

WEATHER:

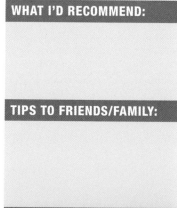

WHERE I WENT:

WHERE I STAYED:

WHO I WENT WITH:

FAVORITE MOMENT:

BEST DRIVING OR WALKING TOUR:

WHAT I'D RECOMMEND:

TIPS TO FRIENDS/FAMILY:

WHAT I WISH I KNEW BEFORE GOING:

WHAT WAS THE FIRST THING I NOTICED WHEN I ARRIVED?

MY FAVORITE PART OF THE VISIT WAS . . .

HOW I SPENT MY TIME THERE:

WHAT WOULD I DO IF I GO BACK?

WHAT IS SOMETHING I LEARNED THERE?

MY TOP THREE FAVORITE ACTIVITIES WERE . . .

1.

2.

3

MY TRIP WAS

/10

JAN   FEB   MAR   APR   MAY   JUN   JUL   AUG   SEP   OCT   NOV   DEC
1 2 3 4 5 6 7 8 9 10 11 12 13 14 15 16 17 18 19 20 21 22 23 24 25 26 27 28 29 30 31

New Mexico

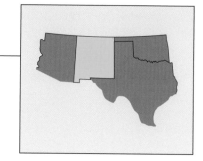

STATE CAPITAL: Santa Fe | **POPULATION:** 2,113,344 *(July 2022)*
STATE NICKNAME: The Land of Enchantment | **YEAR OF STATE-HOOD:** 1912 | **FUN FACT:** The Cathedral Basilica of St. Francis of Assisi in Santa Fe contains the oldest Madonna on U.S. soil.

MAIN ATTRACTIONS:

CITIES: Albuquerque, Clovis, Farmington, Las Cruces, Rio Rancho, Roswell, Santa Fe, Taos

LANDSCAPES: Bandelier National Monument, Carlsbad Caverns National Park, Chaco Culture National Historical Park, El Morro National Monument, Rio Grande del Norte National Monument, Sandia Mountains, Sangre de Cristo Mountains, Shiprock, White Sands National Park

POINTS OF INTEREST: Abiquiú, Acoma Sky City, Bradbury Science Museum, Canyon Road, Cathedral Basilica of St. Francis of Assisi, International Folk Art Market, Kit Carson House/Museum, Loretto Chapel, Los Alamos History Museum, Museum Hill, New Mexico History Museum, Old Town Plaza in Albuquerque, Palace of the Governors, Ranch School's Ice House Memorial, Santa Fe Opera, Taos Pueblo, Trinity Site, White Sands Missile Range

DATE VISITED:

WEATHER:

WHERE I WENT:

WHERE I STAYED:

WHO I WENT WITH:

FAVORITE MOMENT:

BEST DRIVING OR WALKING TOUR:

WHAT I'D RECOMMEND:

TIPS TO FRIENDS/FAMILY:

WHAT I WISH I KNEW BEFORE GOING:

WHAT WAS THE FIRST THING I NOTICED WHEN I ARRIVED?

MY FAVORITE PART OF THE VISIT WAS . . .

HOW I SPENT MY TIME THERE:

WHAT WOULD I DO IF I GO BACK?

WHAT IS SOMETHING I LEARNED THERE?

MY TOP THREE FAVORITE ACTIVITIES WERE . . .

1.

2.

3

MY TRIP WAS

/10

JAN   FEB   MAR   APR   MAY   JUN   JUL   AUG   SEP   OCT   NOV   DEC

1 2 3 4 5 6 7 8 9 10 11 12 13 14 15 16 17 18 19 20 21 22 23 24 25 26 27 28 29 30 31

New York

STATE CAPITAL: Albany | **POPULATION:** 19,677,151 *(July 2022)*
STATE NICKNAME: The Empire State | **YEAR OF STATEHOOD:** 1788
FUN FACT: The Walkway Over the Hudson bridge in Poughkeepsie is the world's longest pedestrian bridge, reaching 6,768 feet.

MAIN ATTRACTIONS:

CITIES: Albany, Alexandria Bay, Buffalo, Canandaigua, Cooperstown, Hunter, Ithaca, New York City, Niagara Falls, Rochester, Syracuse

LANDSCAPES: Adirondack Park, Catskill Mountains, Central Park, Finger Lakes, Hudson River, Lake Champlain, Lake George, Long Island, Montauk, Niagara Falls, Oyster Bay, Sag Harbor, Watkins Glen State Park

POINTS OF INTEREST: 9/11 Memorial & Museum, American Museum of Natural History, Apollo Theater, Bronx Zoo, Brooklyn Bridge, Buffalo AKG Art Museum, Chrysler Building, Coney Island, Empire State Building, Erie Canal Museum, Fort Ticonderoga, High Line, Intrepid Sea, Air & Space Museum, Madison Square Garden, The Metropolitan Museum of Art NY, New York Botanical Garden, One World Trade Center, Radio City Music Hall, Rockefeller Center, Statue of Liberty, Times Square

DATE VISITED:

WEATHER:

WHERE I WENT:

WHERE I STAYED:

WHO I WENT WITH:

FAVORITE MOMENT:

BEST DRIVING OR WALKING TOUR:

WHAT I'D RECOMMEND:

TIPS TO FRIENDS/FAMILY:

WHAT I WISH I KNEW BEFORE GOING:

WHAT WAS THE FIRST THING I NOTICED WHEN I ARRIVED?

**MY FAVORITE PART OF
THE VISIT WAS . . .**

HOW I SPENT MY TIME THERE:

WHAT WOULD I DO IF I GO BACK?

WHAT IS SOMETHING I LEARNED THERE?

MY TOP THREE FAVORITE ACTIVITIES WERE . . .

1.

2.

3

MY TRIP WAS

JAN	FEB	MAR	APR	MAY	JUN	JUL	AUG	SEP	OCT	NOV	DEC
1 2 3	4 5 6	7 8 9	10 11 12	13 14 15	16 17	18 19 20	21 22	23 24 25	26 27	28 29	30 31

North Carolina

STATE CAPITAL: Raleigh | **POPULATION:** 10,698,973 *(July 2022)*
STATE NICKNAME: The Tar Heel State | **YEAR OF STATEHOOD:** 1789
FUN FACT: In 1799, a 12-year-old boy came across gold for the very first time in North America in what became the Reed Gold Mine in Midland.

MAIN ATTRACTIONS:

CITIES: Asheville, Bryson City, Chapel Hill, Charlotte, Durham, Greensboro, Hickory, Kill Devil Hills, Manteo, Midland, Raleigh, Wilmington, Winston-Salem

LANDSCAPES: Appalachians, Cape Fear River, Cape Hatteras National Seashore, Cape Lookout National Seashore, Chimney Rock State Park, French Broad River, Grandfather Mountain, Great Smoky Mountains National Park, Hickory Nut Gorge, Outer Banks, Pisgah National Forest

POINTS OF INTEREST: Asheville's River Arts District, Battleship North Carolina, Bellamy Mansion Museum, Biltmore Estate, Cape Fear Museum, Charlotte Motor Speedway, The Children's Museum of Wilmington, Harvey B. Gantt Center for African-American Arts + Culture, Hendrick Motorsports, Mint Museum Randolph, NASCAR Hall of Fame, North Carolina Aquariums, The North Carolina Arboretum, Poplar Grove Plantation, Southern Highland Craft Guild's Folk Art Center, Wright Brothers National Memorial

DATE VISITED:

WEATHER:

WHERE I WENT:

WHERE I STAYED:

WHO I WENT WITH:

FAVORITE MOMENT:

BEST DRIVING OR WALKING TOUR:

WHAT I'D RECOMMEND:

TIPS TO FRIENDS/FAMILY:

WHAT I WISH I KNEW BEFORE GOING:

WHAT WAS THE FIRST THING I NOTICED WHEN I ARRIVED?

MY FAVORITE PART OF THE VISIT WAS . . .

HOW I SPENT MY TIME THERE:

WHAT WOULD I DO IF I GO BACK?

WHAT IS SOMETHING I LEARNED THERE?

MY TOP THREE FAVORITE ACTIVITIES WERE . . .

1.

2.

3

MY TRIP WAS

/10

JAN   FEB   MAR   APR   MAY   JUN   JUL   AUG   SEP   OCT   NOV   DEC

1 2 3 4 5 6 7 8 9 10 11 12 13 14 15 16 17 18 19 20 21 22 23 24 25 26 27 28 29 30 31

North Dakota

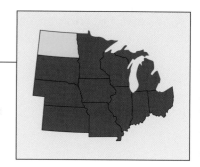

STATE CAPITAL: Bismarck | **POPULATION:** 779,261 *(July 2022)*
STATE NICKNAME: The Peace Garden State | **YEAR OF STATEHOOD:**
1889 | **FUN FACT:** The National Buffalo Museum is home to the World's
Largest Buffalo monument, standing at 26 feet tall and weighing 60 tons.

MAIN ATTRACTIONS:

CITIES: Bismarck, Cooperstown, Fargo, Grand Forks, Jamestown, Medora, Minot

LANDSCAPES: Fort Abraham Lincoln State Park, Knife River Indian Villages National
Historic Site, Little Missouri National Grassland, Red River, Theodore Roosevelt
National Park

POINTS OF INTEREST: Camp Hancock State Historic Site, Chateau de Mores,
Dakota Territory Air Museum, Dakota Zoo, Elkhorn Ranch, Eugene Dahl Car Museum
at Bonanzaville, Fargo Air Museum, Fort Abraham Lincoln Custer House, High Line
Bridge, International Peace Garden, Lewis & Clark Interpretive Center, National Buffalo
Museum, North Dakota Heritage Center & State Museum, North Dakota Museum of
Art, Plains Art Museum, Red River Zoo, Minot Air Force Base, Theodore Roosevelt's
Maltese Cross Cabin

DATE VISITED:

WEATHER:

WHERE I WENT:

WHERE I STAYED:

WHO I WENT WITH:

FAVORITE MOMENT:

BEST DRIVING OR WALKING TOUR:

WHAT I'D RECOMMEND:

TIPS TO FRIENDS/FAMILY:

WHAT I WISH I KNEW BEFORE GOING:

WHAT WAS THE FIRST THING I NOTICED WHEN I ARRIVED?

MY FAVORITE PART OF THE VISIT WAS . . .

HOW I SPENT MY TIME THERE:

WHAT WOULD I DO IF I GO BACK?

WHAT IS SOMETHING I LEARNED THERE?

MY TOP THREE FAVORITE ACTIVITIES WERE . . .

1.

2.

3

MY TRIP WAS

10

JAN   FEB   MAR   APR   MAY   JUN   JUL   AUG   SEP   OCT   NOV   DEC
1   2   3   4   5   6   7   8   9   10   11   12   13   14   15   16   17   18   19   20   21   22   23   24   25   26   27   28   29   30   31

Northern Mariana Islands

TERRITORY CAPITAL: Capital Hill | **POPULATION:** 51,295 *(April 2023)*
TERRITORY NICKNAME: America's Best Kept Secret | **YEAR OF**
U.S. TERRITORYHOOD: 1975 | **FUN FACT:** The stone structures with
crescent-shaped tops, known as latte stones, found all over the islands
are actually ancient support pillars.

MAIN ATTRACTIONS:

ISLANDS: Aguijan, Farallon de Medinilla, Guguan, Rota, Saipan, Tinian

LANDSCAPES: American Memorial Park, Bird Island, Chugai' Pictograph Site,
Kalabera Cave, Micro Beach, Mount Lasso, Mount Sabana, Mount Taipingot, Mount
Tapochau, Obyan Beach, Old Man by the Sea Beach, Pau Pau Beach, Sasanhaya
Bay, Taga Beach

POINTS OF INTEREST: Atomic Bomb Loading Pits, Capital Hill, Chalan Kanoa Village,
l'Chenchon Park Bird Sanctuary, Cliff Fishing Derby, Forbidden Island, Garapan Central
Park, Garapan's Kristo Rai Catholic Church, Garapan Street Market, the Grotto, House
of Taga, Mochong Latte Site, Northern Mariana Islands Museum of History & Culture,
Old Japanese Cannon, Our Lady of Mount Carmel Cathedral, Pona Point Fishing Cliff,
Puntan Carolinas, Saipan Beach Road Pathway

DATE VISITED:

WEATHER:

WHERE I WENT:

WHERE I STAYED:

WHO I WENT WITH:

FAVORITE MOMENT:

BEST DRIVING OR WALKING TOUR:

WHAT I'D RECOMMEND:

TIPS TO FRIENDS/FAMILY:

WHAT I WISH I KNEW BEFORE GOING:

WHAT WAS THE FIRST THING I NOTICED WHEN I ARRIVED?

MY FAVORITE PART OF THE VISIT WAS . . .

HOW I SPENT MY TIME THERE:

WHAT WOULD I DO IF I GO BACK?

WHAT IS SOMETHING I LEARNED THERE?

MY TOP THREE FAVORITE ACTIVITIES WERE . . .

1.

2.

3

MY TRIP WAS

/10

JAN   FEB   MAR   APR   MAY   JUN   JUL   AUG   SEP   OCT   NOV   DEC
1 2 3 4 5 6 7 8 9 10 11 12 13 14 15 16 17 18 19 20 21 22 23 24 25 26 27 28 29 30 31

Ohio

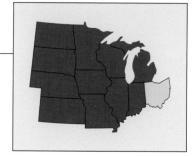

STATE CAPITAL: Columbus | **POPULATION:** 11,756,058 *(July 2022)*
STATE NICKNAME: The Buckeye State | **YEAR OF STATEHOOD:** 1803
FUN FACT: The famous inventor Thomas Edison was born in Milan, Ohio, in 1847.

MAIN ATTRACTIONS:

CITIES: Ashtabula, Cincinnati, Cleveland, Columbus, Dayton, Jefferson, Marblehead, Toledo, Warren, Youngstown

LANDSCAPES: Allegheny Plateau, Cuyahoga Valley National Park, Hocking Hills, Lake Erie Archipelago, Serpent Mound meteor crater

POINTS OF INTEREST: *A Christmas Story* House & Museum, the Amish & Mennonite Heritage Center, Cincinnati Zoo & Botanical Garden, Cleveland Botanical Garden, Cleveland Museum of Natural History, Columbus Museum of Art, Geneva-on-the-Lake, Great Lakes Science Center, Historic Roscoe Village, John A. Roebling Bridge, Marblehead Lighthouse, National Museum of the U.S. Air Force, Over-the-Rhine district in Cincinnati, Pro Football Hall of Fame, Rock & Roll Hall of Fame, Severance Music Center, Smolen-Gulf Bridge, Steamship *William G. Mather,* Thurber House, Toledo Museum of Art's Glass Pavilion, U.S.S. *Cod* Submarine Memorial

DATE VISITED:

WEATHER:

WHERE I WENT:

WHERE I STAYED:

WHO I WENT WITH:

FAVORITE MOMENT:

BEST DRIVING OR WALKING TOUR:

WHAT I'D RECOMMEND:

TIPS TO FRIENDS/FAMILY:

WHAT I WISH I KNEW BEFORE GOING:

WHAT WAS THE FIRST THING I NOTICED WHEN I ARRIVED?

MY FAVORITE PART OF THE VISIT WAS . . .

HOW I SPENT MY TIME THERE:

WHAT WOULD I DO IF I GO BACK?

WHAT IS SOMETHING I LEARNED THERE?

MY TOP THREE FAVORITE ACTIVITIES WERE . . .

1.

2.

3

MY TRIP WAS

JAN   FEB   MAR   APR   MAY   JUN   JUL   AUG   SEP   OCT   NOV   DEC
1   2   3   4   5   6   7   8   9   10   11   12   13   14   15   16   17   18   19   20   21   22   23   24   25   26   27   28   29   30   31

Oklahoma

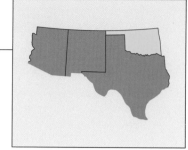

STATE CAPITAL: Oklahoma City | **POPULATION:** 4,019,800 *(July 2022)*
STATE NICKNAME: The Sooner State | **YEAR OF STATEHOOD:** 1907
FUN FACT: Oklahoma's original state flag was replaced in 1925 because it too closely resembled a communist banner.

MAIN ATTRACTIONS:

CITIES: Broken Arrow, Claremore, Elk City, Hugo, Idabel, Medicine Park, Norman, Oklahoma City, Oologah, Sulphur, Tahlequah, Tulsa, Wewoka, Yale

LANDSCAPES: Arbuckle Mountains, Black Kettle National Grassland, Chickasaw National Recreation Area, Quartz Mountain State Park, Turners Falls, Spiro Mounds, Wichita Mountains

POINTS OF INTEREST: Chickasaw Cultural Center, Crystal Bridge Tropical Conservatory, Devon Energy Center, Elk City's Route 66 & Transportation Museum, Fort Reno, Fred Jones Jr. Museum of Art, Myriad Botanical Gardens, National Cowboy & Western Heritage Museum, Oklahoma City National Memorial & Museum, Oklahoma City Zoo, Oklahoma Route 66 Museum, Sam Noble Museum, Stafford Air & Space Museum, Will Rogers Memorial Museum & Birthplace Ranch, Woody Guthrie Center

DATE VISITED:

WEATHER:

WHERE I WENT:

WHERE I STAYED:

WHO I WENT WITH:

FAVORITE MOMENT:

BEST DRIVING OR WALKING TOUR:

WHAT I'D RECOMMEND:

TIPS TO FRIENDS/FAMILY:

WHAT I WISH I KNEW BEFORE GOING:

WHAT WAS THE FIRST THING I NOTICED WHEN I ARRIVED?

MY FAVORITE PART OF THE VISIT WAS . . .

HOW I SPENT MY TIME THERE:

WHAT WOULD I DO IF I GO BACK?

WHAT IS SOMETHING I LEARNED THERE?

MY TOP THREE FAVORITE ACTIVITIES WERE . . .

1.

2.

3

MY TRIP WAS

JAN   FEB   MAR   APR   MAY   JUN   JUL   AUG   SEP   OCT   NOV   DEC
1 2 3 4 5 6 7 8 9 10 11 12 13 14 15 16 17 18 19 20 21 22 23 24 25 26 27 28 29 30 31

....

....

....

....

....

....

....

....

....

....

....

....

....

....

....

....

....

....

....

....

....

....

Oregon

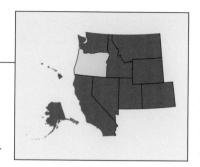

STATE CAPITAL: Salem | **POPULATION:** 4,240,137 *(July 2022)*
STATE NICKNAME: The Beaver State | **YEAR OF STATEHOOD:** 1859
FUN FACT: Oregon Dunes National Recreation Area has the largest expanse of coastal sand dunes in North America, with some dunes ascending 500 feet.

MAIN ATTRACTIONS:

CITIES: Ashland, Astoria, Baker City, Bend, Cannon Beach, Eugene, Gresham, Newport, Portland, Salem

LANDSCAPES: Cascade Range, Columbia River, Columbia River Gorge National Scenic Area, Crater Lake National Park, Ecola State Park, Hells Canyon National Recreation Area, Mount Hood, Oregon Caves National Monument & Preserve, Siskiyou Mountains, Snake River, Willamette Valley, Yaquina Bay State Park, Yaquina Head Outstanding Natural Area

POINTS OF INTEREST: Arlene Schnitzer Concert Hall, Cascades Raptor Center, Governor Tom McCall Waterfront Park, Hoyt Arboretum, Lewis and Clark National Historical Park, Lincoln Hall, National Historic Oregon Trail Interpretive Center, Oregon Coast Aquarium, Oregon Dunes National Recreation Area, Oregon Historical Society Museum, Oregon Maritime Museum, Oregon Museum of Science and Industry, Portland Art Museum, Portland Japanese Garden, Washington Park

DATE VISITED:

WEATHER:

WHERE I WENT:

WHERE I STAYED:

WHO I WENT WITH:

FAVORITE MOMENT:

BEST DRIVING OR WALKING TOUR:

WHAT I'D RECOMMEND:

TIPS TO FRIENDS/FAMILY:

WHAT I WISH I KNEW BEFORE GOING:

WHAT WAS THE FIRST THING I NOTICED WHEN I ARRIVED?

MY FAVORITE PART OF THE VISIT WAS . . .

HOW I SPENT MY TIME THERE:

WHAT WOULD I DO IF I GO BACK?

WHAT IS SOMETHING I LEARNED THERE?

MY TOP THREE FAVORITE ACTIVITIES WERE . . .

1.

2.

3

MY TRIP WAS

10

JAN   FEB   MAR   APR   MAY   JUN   JUL   AUG   SEP   OCT   NOV   DEC
1 2 3   4 5 6   7 8 9   10 11   12   13 14   15 16 17   18 19   20 21 22   23 24   25 26 27   28 29   30 31

Pennsylvania

STATE CAPITAL: Harrisburg | **POPULATION:** 12,972,008 *(July 2022)*
STATE NICKNAME: The Keystone State | **YEAR OF STATEHOOD:** 1787
FUN FACT: The nation's largest chocolate factory was completed in 1905 by Milton S. Hershey. Hershey, Pennsylvania, is now a mecca for chocolate lovers.

MAIN ATTRACTIONS:

CITIES: Harrisburg, Hershey, Lancaster, Philadelphia, Pittsburgh, Williamsport, Youngsville

LANDSCAPES: Pennsylvania Wilds, Presque Isle State Park

POINTS OF INTEREST: Allegheny Reservoir, The Andy Warhol Museum, Betsy Ross House, Carnegie Museums of Pittsburgh, Christ Church Burial Ground, Duquesne Incline funicular railway, Flight 93 National Memorial, Frank Lloyd Wright's Fallingwater, The Frick Collection, Gettysburg National Military Park, Heinz Memorial Chapel, Independence National Historical Park, Independence Seaport Museum, Johnstown Flood National Memorial, Liberty Bell Center, Longwood Gardens, National Constitution Center, Penn's Landing, Pennsylvania Dutch Country, Philadelphia's Magic Gardens, Philadelphia Museum of Art, Phipps Conservatory and Botanical Gardens, Valley Forge National Historical Park, Weitzman National Museum of American Jewish History, ZooAmerica

DATE VISITED:

WEATHER:

WHERE I WENT:

WHERE I STAYED:

WHO I WENT WITH:

FAVORITE MOMENT:

BEST DRIVING OR WALKING TOUR:

WHAT I'D RECOMMEND:

TIPS TO FRIENDS/FAMILY:

WHAT I WISH I KNEW BEFORE GOING:

WHAT WAS THE FIRST THING I NOTICED WHEN I ARRIVED?

MY FAVORITE PART OF THE VISIT WAS . . .

HOW I SPENT MY TIME THERE:

WHAT WOULD I DO IF I GO BACK?

WHAT IS SOMETHING I LEARNED THERE?

MY TOP THREE FAVORITE ACTIVITIES WERE . . .

1.

2.

3

MY TRIP WAS

/10

JAN   FEB   MAR   APR   MAY   JUN   JUL   AUG   SEP   OCT   NOV   DEC
1 2 3 4 5 6 7 8 9 10 11 12 13 14 15 16 17 18 19 20 21 22 23 24 25 26 27 28 29 30 31

....

....

....

....

....

....

....

....

....

....

....

....

....

....

....

....

....

....

....

....

....

Puerto Rico

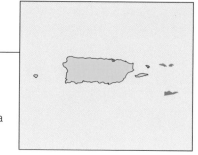

TERRITORY CAPITAL: San Juan | **POPULATION:** 3,221,789 (*July 2022*) | **TERRITORY NICKNAME:** Isla del Encanto (Island of Enchantment) | **YEAR OF U.S. TERRITORYHOOD:** 1917 | **FUN FACT:** The piña colada is the official drink of Puerto Rico, though there is debate over the original recipe and who created it.

MAIN ATTRACTIONS:

CITIES: Arecibo, Caguas, Dorado, Fajardo, Ponce, Río Grande, San Juan, Vieques

LANDSCAPES: Black Sand Beach, Cabezas de San Juan Nature Reserve, Cabo Rojo's salt flats, El Yunque National Forest, Flamenco Beach, Isla Caja de Muertos, Lago Dos Bocas, Monte Pirata, Mosquito Bioluminescent Bay, Playa Mar Chiquita, Reserva Natural Cayos de la Cordillera, Río Camuy Cave Park, Río Grande de Loíza, Sierra de Luquillo, Tanamá River, Vieques National Wildlife Refuge

POINTS OF INTEREST: Casa BACARDÍ, Castillo San Cristobal, Centro Cultural Carmen Solá de Pereira de Ponce, Museo de Arte de Ponce, Museo de Arte y Diseño de Miramar, Playa Escondida, Plaza del Mercado en Santurce, Plaza las Delicias, San Juan National Historic Site, Toro Verde Nature Adventure Park

DATE VISITED:

WEATHER:

WHERE I WENT:

WHERE I STAYED:

WHO I WENT WITH:

FAVORITE MOMENT:

BEST DRIVING OR WALKING TOUR:

WHAT I'D RECOMMEND:

TIPS TO FRIENDS/FAMILY:

WHAT I WISH I KNEW BEFORE GOING:

WHAT WAS THE FIRST THING I NOTICED WHEN I ARRIVED?

MY FAVORITE PART OF THE VISIT WAS . . .

HOW I SPENT MY TIME THERE:

WHAT WOULD I DO IF I GO BACK?

WHAT IS SOMETHING I LEARNED THERE?

MY TOP THREE FAVORITE ACTIVITIES WERE . . .

1.

2.

3

MY TRIP WAS

/10

JAN   FEB   MAR   APR   MAY   JUN   JUL   AUG   SEP   OCT   NOV   DEC
1   2   3   4   5   6   7   8   9   10   11   12   13   14   15   16   17   18   19   20   21   22   23   24   25   26   27   28   29   30   31

Rhode Island

STATE CAPITAL: Providence | **POPULATION:** 1,093,734 *(July 2022)*
STATE NICKNAME: The Ocean State | **YEAR OF STATEHOOD:** 1790
FUN FACT: The nation's oldest Jewish temple, Touro Synagogue, was founded in 1763 in Newport.

MAIN ATTRACTIONS:

CITIES: Bristol, Newport, Little Compton, Narragansett, New Shoreham, Pawtucket, Providence, South Kingstown, Warwick, Woonsocket

LANDSCAPES: Blackstone River State Park, Block Island National Wildlife Refuge, Fort Adams State Park, Great Salt Pond, Mohegan Bluffs, Napatree Point Conservation Area, Narragansett Bay, Providence River, Roger W. Wheeler State Beach, South Shore Beach, Woonasquatucket River

POINTS OF INTEREST: Albion River Bridge, Beavertail Lighthouse Museum, Blackstone River Valley National Heritage Corridor, Blithewold Estate, Bowen's Wharf, Brown University, Cliff Walk, Herreshoff Marine Museum & America's Cup Hall of Fame, International Tennis Hall of Fame, the John Brown House Museum, Manisses Animal Farm, Newport Harbor, Old Slater Mill, Providence Performing Arts Center, Providence Place, Rhode Island School of Design Museum, Southeast Lighthouse, WaterFire Arts Center

DATE VISITED:

WEATHER:

WHERE I WENT:

WHERE I STAYED:

WHO I WENT WITH:

FAVORITE MOMENT:

BEST DRIVING OR WALKING TOUR:

WHAT I'D RECOMMEND:

TIPS TO FRIENDS/FAMILY:

WHAT I WISH I KNEW BEFORE GOING:

WHAT WAS THE FIRST THING I NOTICED WHEN I ARRIVED?

MY FAVORITE PART OF THE VISIT WAS . . .

HOW I SPENT MY TIME THERE:

WHAT WOULD I DO IF I GO BACK?

WHAT IS SOMETHING I LEARNED THERE?

MY TOP THREE FAVORITE ACTIVITIES WERE . . .

1.

2.

3

MY TRIP WAS

/10

JAN   FEB   MAR   APR   MAY   JUN   JUL   AUG   SEP   OCT   NOV   DEC
1   2   3   4   5   6   7   8   9   10   11   12   13   14   15   16   17   18   19   20   21   22   23   24   25   26   27   28   29   30   31

South Carolina

STATE CAPITAL: Columbia | **POPULATION:** 5,282,634 (*July 2022*)
STATE NICKNAME: The Palmetto State | **YEAR OF STATEHOOD:** 1788
FUN FACT: More than 4,000 rhesus monkeys roam freely on Morgan Island, the only place where they do so in the U.S.

MAIN ATTRACTIONS:

CITIES: Beaufort, Charleston, Columbia, Hardeeville, Hilton Head Island, Myrtle Beach

LANDSCAPES: Ashley River, Broad River, Caesars Head State Park, Congaree National Park, Cooper River, Jones Gap State Park, Lowcountry, Mountain Bridge Wilderness Area, Pinckney Island National Wildlife Refuge, Raven Cliff Falls, Saluda River, Sea Islands

POINTS OF INTEREST: South Carolina Aquarium, the Battery, Boone Hall Plantation & Gardens, Williams Mansion, Arts Center of Coastal Carolina, Charles Towne Landing State Historic Site, The Charleston Museum, Fort Sumter and Fort Moultrie National Historical Park, John Mark Verdier House, Magnolia Plantation & Gardens, Middleton Place, Patriots Point Naval & Maritime Museum, Ripley's Aquarium of Myrtle Beach, Riverbanks Zoo & Garden, South Carolina State Museum, White Point Garden

DATE VISITED:

WEATHER:

WHERE I WENT:

WHERE I STAYED:

WHO I WENT WITH:

FAVORITE MOMENT:

BEST DRIVING OR WALKING TOUR:

WHAT I'D RECOMMEND:

TIPS TO FRIENDS/FAMILY:

WHAT I WISH I KNEW BEFORE GOING:

WHAT WAS THE FIRST THING I NOTICED WHEN I ARRIVED?

MY FAVORITE PART OF THE VISIT WAS . . .

HOW I SPENT MY TIME THERE:

WHAT WOULD I DO IF I GO BACK?

WHAT IS SOMETHING I LEARNED THERE?

MY TOP THREE FAVORITE ACTIVITIES WERE . . .

1.

2.

3

MY TRIP WAS

10

JAN   FEB   MAR   APR   MAY   JUN   JUL   AUG   SEP   OCT   NOV   DEC
1 2 3 4 5 6 7 8 9 10 11 12 13 14 15 16 17 18 19 20 21 22 23 24 25 26 27 28 29 30 31

....

....

....

....

....

....

....

....

....

....

....

....

....

....

....

....

....

....

....

....

....

South Dakota

STATE CAPITAL: Pierre | **POPULATION:** 909,824 *(July 2022)* | **STATE NICKNAME:** The Mount Rushmore State | **YEAR OF STATEHOOD:** 1889
FUN FACT: Sturgis is renowned for the world's largest annual gathering of motorcycle enthusiasts; it was first staged in 1938.

MAIN ATTRACTIONS:

CITIES: Deadwood, De Smet, Hot Springs, Pierre, Rapid City, Sioux Falls, Sturgis, Wessington Springs

LANDSCAPES: Badlands National Park, Black Hills, Custer State Park, Good Earth State Park, Jewel Cave National Monument, Wind Cave National Park

POINTS OF INTEREST: Broken Boot Gold Mine, Butterfly House & Aquarium, Crazy Horse Memorial, Dahl Arts Center, Cyclorama of American Economic History mural, Great Plains Zoo & Delbridge Museum of Natural History, Homestake Adams Research and Cultural Center, Indian Museum of North America, Minuteman Missile National Historic Site, Mount Rushmore National Memorial, National Presidential Wax Museum, Old Courthouse Museum, Pettigrew Home & Museum, Prairie Village, Sturgis Motorcycle Rally

DATE VISITED:

WEATHER:

WHERE I WENT:

WHERE I STAYED:

WHO I WENT WITH:

FAVORITE MOMENT:

BEST DRIVING OR WALKING TOUR:

WHAT I'D RECOMMEND:

TIPS TO FRIENDS/FAMILY:

WHAT I WISH I KNEW BEFORE GOING:

WHAT WAS THE FIRST THING I NOTICED WHEN I ARRIVED?

**MY FAVORITE PART OF
THE VISIT WAS . . .**

HOW I SPENT MY TIME THERE:

WHAT WOULD I DO IF I GO BACK?

WHAT IS SOMETHING I LEARNED THERE?

MY TOP THREE FAVORITE ACTIVITIES WERE . . .

1.

2.

3

MY TRIP WAS

/10

JAN   FEB   MAR   APR   MAY   JUN   JUL   AUG   SEP   OCT   NOV   DEC
1 2 3 4 5 6 7 8 9 10 11 12 13 14 15 16 17 18 19 20 21 22 23 24 25 26 27 28 29 30 31

Tennessee

STATE CAPITAL: Nashville | **POPULATION:** 7,051,339 *(July 2022)*
STATE NICKNAME: The Volunteer State | **YEAR OF STATEHOOD:** 1796
FUN FACT: Memphis was named after an ancient Egyptian city.

MAIN ATTRACTIONS:

CITIES: Chattanooga, Franklin, Gatlinburg, Harrogate, Jonesborough, Knoxville, Manchester, Memphis, Nashville, Pigeon Forge

LANDSCAPES: Cades Cove, Cumberland River, Great Smoky Mountains National Park, Lookout Mountain, Raccoon Mountain Caverns, Rock City Gardens, Ruby Falls, Sugarlands Distilling Company

POINTS OF INTEREST: Andrew Jackson's Hermitage, Beale Street, Belle Meade Historic Site & Winery, Bonnaroo Music & Arts Festival, Cooter's Place, Country Music Hall of Fame and Museum, Dollywood, Grand Ole Opry, Hunter Museum of American Art, Memphis Rock 'n' Soul Museum, Moccasin Bend National Archeological District, National Civil Rights Museum, Oak Ridge National Laboratory, Ryman Auditorium, Shiloh National Military Park, Stax Museum of American Soul Music, Tennessee Aquarium

DATE VISITED:

WEATHER:

WHERE I WENT:

WHERE I STAYED:

WHO I WENT WITH:

FAVORITE MOMENT:

BEST DRIVING OR WALKING TOUR:

WHAT I'D RECOMMEND:

TIPS TO FRIENDS/FAMILY:

WHAT I WISH I KNEW BEFORE GOING:

WHAT WAS THE FIRST THING I NOTICED WHEN I ARRIVED?

**MY FAVORITE PART OF
THE VISIT WAS . . .**

HOW I SPENT MY TIME THERE:

WHAT WOULD I DO IF I GO BACK?

WHAT IS SOMETHING I LEARNED THERE?

MY TOP THREE FAVORITE ACTIVITIES WERE . . .

1.

2.

3

MY TRIP WAS

10

JAN   FEB   MAR   APR   MAY   JUN   JUL   AUG   SEP   OCT   NOV   DEC
1 2 3 4 5 6 7 8 9 10 11 12 13 14 15 16 17 18 19 20 21 22 23 24 25 26 27 28 29 30 31

Texas

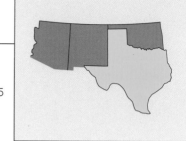

STATE CAPITAL: Austin | **POPULATION:** 30,029,572 *(July 2022)*
STATE NICKNAME: The Lone Star State | **YEAR OF STATEHOOD:** 1845
FUN FACT: Houston is home to the world's largest medical complex, Texas Medical Center.

MAIN ATTRACTIONS:

CITIES: Amarillo, Austin, Burnet, Dallas, El Paso, Fort Worth, Galveston, Houston, San Antonio

LANDSCAPES: Big Bend National Park, Guadalupe Mountains National Park, Gulf Coast, Hueco Tanks State Park & Historic Site, Longhorn Cavern State Park, Lost Maples State Natural Area, Padre Island National Seashore, Palo Duro Canyon State Park, Rio Grande

POINTS OF INTEREST: The Alamo site, Amon Carter Museum of American Art, Elisabet Ney Museum, Fort Worth Botanic Garden, Fort Worth Stockyards National Historic District, Klyde Warren Park, Lady Bird Johnson Wildflower Center, Modern Art Museum of Fort Worth, Morton H. Meyerson Symphony Center, NASA's Johnson Space Center, Nasher Sculpture Center, The Sixth Floor Museum at Dealey Plaza, San Antonio River Walk

DATE VISITED:

WEATHER:

WHERE I WENT:

WHERE I STAYED:

WHO I WENT WITH:

FAVORITE MOMENT:

BEST DRIVING OR WALKING TOUR:

WHAT I'D RECOMMEND:

TIPS TO FRIENDS/FAMILY:

WHAT I WISH I KNEW BEFORE GOING:

WHAT WAS THE FIRST THING I NOTICED WHEN I ARRIVED?

MY FAVORITE PART OF THE VISIT WAS . . .

HOW I SPENT MY TIME THERE:

WHAT WOULD I DO IF I GO BACK?

WHAT IS SOMETHING I LEARNED THERE?

MY TOP THREE FAVORITE ACTIVITIES WERE . . .

1.

2.

3

MY TRIP WAS

/10

U.S. Virgin Islands

TERRITORY CAPITAL: Charlotte Amalie | **POPULATION:** 104,917 *(April 2023)* | **TERRITORY NICKNAME:** America's Paradise | **YEAR OF U.S. TERRITORYHOOD:** 1917 | **FUN FACT:** Point Udall on St. Croix is the easternmost point (by travel, not longitude) of the U.S.

MAIN ATTRACTIONS:

ISLANDS: St. John, St. Thomas, St. Croix

CITIES: Charlotte Amalie, Christiansted, Frederiksted, Frenchtown

LANDSCAPES: Cinnamon Bay, Hans Lollik Islands, Lindqvist Beach, Magens Bay, Point Udall, Sandy Point National Wildlife Refuge, Virgin Islands National Park

POINTS OF INTEREST: Adventures in Diving STX, Agrifest, Caribbean Museum Center for the Arts, Coki Beach, Coral World Ocean Park, Estate La Reine, Fort Christian, Franklin A. Powell Sr. Park, 99 Steps in Charlotte Amalie, Phantasea Tropical Botanical Garden, Pirates Treasure Museum, Rothschild Francis Square, St. John Brewers on the Waterfront, Skyride to Paradise Point, Tree Limin' Extreme Zipline, the Virgin Islands Children's Museum

DATE VISITED:

WEATHER:

WHERE I WENT:

WHERE I STAYED:

WHO I WENT WITH:

FAVORITE MOMENT:

BEST DRIVING OR WALKING TOUR:

WHAT I'D RECOMMEND:

TIPS TO FRIENDS/FAMILY:

WHAT I WISH I KNEW BEFORE GOING:

WHAT WAS THE FIRST THING I NOTICED WHEN I ARRIVED?

MY FAVORITE PART OF THE VISIT WAS . . .

HOW I SPENT MY TIME THERE:

WHAT WOULD I DO IF I GO BACK?

WHAT IS SOMETHING I LEARNED THERE?

MY TOP THREE FAVORITE ACTIVITIES WERE . . .

1.

2.

3

MY TRIP WAS

10

JAN	FEB	MAR	APR	MAY	JUN	JUL	AUG	SEP	OCT	NOV	DEC

1 2 3 4 5 6 7 8 9 10 11 12 13 14 15 16 17 18 19 20 21 22 23 24 25 26 27 28 29 30 31

Utah

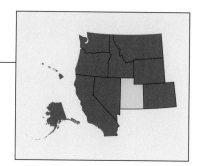

STATE CAPITAL: Salt Lake City | **POPULATION:** 3,380,800 *(July 2022)*
STATE NICKNAME: The Beehive State | **YEAR OF STATEHOOD:** 1896
FUN FACT: Park City Mountain ski resort makes up the nation's largest concentration of lifts and skiable terrain.

MAIN ATTRACTIONS:

CITIES: Cedar City, Moab, Ogden, Park City, Provo, Salt Lake City, Springdale

LANDSCAPES: Antelope Island State Park, Arches National Park, Bryce Canyon National Park, Canyonlands National Park, Capitol Reef National Park, Cedar Breaks National Monument, Dinosaur National Monument, Glen Canyon National Recreation Area, Great Salt Lake, Monument Valley Navajo Tribal Park, Natural Bridges National Monument, Promontory Summit, Uinta Mountains, Virgin River, Zion National Park

POINTS OF INTEREST: Bumbleberry Theatre, Church History Museum, Discovery Gateway Children's Museum, Easter Jeep Safari, Fort Douglas Military Museum, Golden Spike National Historical Park, O.C. Tanner Amphitheater, Rainbow Bridge National Monument, Salt Lake Temple, Seagull Monument, This Is the Place Heritage Park, Utah Olympic Park, Washington Square in Salt Lake, Zion Human History Museum

DATE VISITED:

WEATHER:

WHERE I WENT:

WHERE I STAYED:

WHO I WENT WITH:

FAVORITE MOMENT:

BEST DRIVING OR WALKING TOUR:

WHAT I'D RECOMMEND:

TIPS TO FRIENDS/FAMILY:

WHAT I WISH I KNEW BEFORE GOING:

WHAT WAS THE FIRST THING I NOTICED WHEN I ARRIVED?

MY FAVORITE PART OF THE VISIT WAS . . .

HOW I SPENT MY TIME THERE:

WHAT WOULD I DO IF I GO BACK?

WHAT IS SOMETHING I LEARNED THERE?

MY TOP THREE FAVORITE ACTIVITIES WERE . . .

1.

2.

3

MY TRIP WAS

JAN   FEB   MAR   APR   MAY   JUN   JUL   AUG   SEP   OCT   NOV   DEC
1 2 3 4 5 6 7 8 9 10 11 12 13 14 15 16 17 18 19 20 21 22 23 24 25 26 27 28 29 30 31

Vermont

STATE CAPITAL: Montpelier **|** **POPULATION:** 647,064 *(July 2022)*
STATE NICKNAME: The Green Mountain State **|** **YEAR OF STATE-HOOD:** 1791 **|** **FUN FACT:** Vermont is the leading producer of maple syrup in the nation.

MAIN ATTRACTIONS:

CITIES: Barre, Bennington, Burlington, Dummerston, Killington, Manchester, Montpelier, Norwich, Shelburne, Stowe, Vergennes, Warren, Woodstock

LANDSCAPES: Coolidge State Park, Green Mountain National Forest, Isle La Motte, Lake Champlain, Lake Champlain Islands, Mount Mansfield, Smugglers' Notch State Park, West River, Winooski River

POINTS OF INTEREST: Bennington Battle Monument, ECHO–Leahy Center for Lake Champlain, Ethan Allen Homestead Museum, Fleming Museum of Art, the Flynn, Gold Brook Covered Bridge, Hyde Log Cabin, Island Line Trail, Kellogg-Hubbard Library, Killington Ski Resort, Lake Champlain Maritime Museum, Lost Nation Theater, Marsh-Billings-Rockefeller National Historical Park, Rock of Ages, Shelburne Museum, Trapp Family Lodge, Vermont History Museum, Vermont Teddy Bear Company, West Dummerston Covered Bridge

DATE VISITED:

WEATHER:

WHERE I WENT:

WHERE I STAYED:

WHO I WENT WITH:

FAVORITE MOMENT:

BEST DRIVING OR WALKING TOUR:

WHAT I'D RECOMMEND:

TIPS TO FRIENDS/FAMILY:

WHAT I WISH I KNEW BEFORE GOING:

WHAT WAS THE FIRST THING I NOTICED WHEN I ARRIVED?

MY FAVORITE PART OF THE VISIT WAS . . .

HOW I SPENT MY TIME THERE:

WHAT WOULD I DO IF I GO BACK?

WHAT IS SOMETHING I LEARNED THERE?

MY TOP THREE FAVORITE ACTIVITIES WERE . . .

1.

2.

3

MY TRIP WAS

JAN   FEB   MAR   APR   MAY   JUN   JUL   AUG   SEP   OCT   NOV   DEC
1   2   3   4   5   6   7   8   9   10   11   12   13   14   15   16   17   18   19   20   21   22   23   24   25   26   27   28   29   30   31

Virginia

STATE CAPITAL: Richmond | **POPULATION:** 8,683,619 *(July 2022)*
STATE NICKNAME: The Old Dominion | **YEAR OF STATEHOOD:** 1788
FUN FACT: The first American Thanksgiving, a 1619 feast between English settlers and local Native Americans, was held at a site on Berkeley Plantation.

MAIN ATTRACTIONS:

CITIES: Alexandria, Appomattox, Arlington, Charlottesville, Clarksville, Fredericksburg, Galax, Hampton, Norfolk, Portsmouth, Richmond, Virginia Beach, Yorktown

LANDSCAPES: Alleghany Highlands, Back Bay National Wildlife Refuge, Blue Ridge Mountains, Chesapeake Bay, Chincoteague National Wildlife Refuge, Cumberland Plateau, Douthat State Park, First Landing State Park, Great Falls Park, Humpback Rocks, Mount Rogers National Recreation Area, Shenandoah National Park, Tangier Island

POINTS OF INTEREST: Arlington National Cemetery, Colonial Williamsburg, Hippodrome Theatre, Jamestown, MacArthur Memorial, Manassas National Battlefield Park, Monticello, Monument Avenue, Mount Vernon, Nauticus, Naval Station Norfolk, Norfolk Botanical Garden, Old Town Alexandria, the Poe Museum, Richmond National Battlefield Park, Smithsonian National Air and Space Museum's Steven F. Udvar-Hazy Center, Virginia Aquarium & Marine Science Center

DATE VISITED:

WEATHER:

WHERE I WENT:

WHERE I STAYED:

WHO I WENT WITH:

FAVORITE MOMENT:

BEST DRIVING OR WALKING TOUR:

WHAT I'D RECOMMEND:

TIPS TO FRIENDS/FAMILY:

WHAT I WISH I KNEW BEFORE GOING:

WHAT WAS THE FIRST THING I NOTICED WHEN I ARRIVED?

**MY FAVORITE PART OF
THE VISIT WAS . . .**

HOW I SPENT MY TIME THERE:

WHAT WOULD I DO IF I GO BACK?

WHAT IS SOMETHING I LEARNED THERE?

MY TOP THREE FAVORITE ACTIVITIES WERE . . .

1.

2.

3

MY TRIP WAS

/10

JAN   FEB   MAR   APR   MAY   JUN   JUL   AUG   SEP   OCT   NOV   DEC
1 2 3 4 5 6 7 8 9 10 11 12 13 14 15 16 17 18 19 20 21 22 23 24 25 26 27 28 29 30 31

Washington

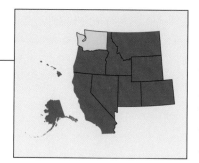

STATE CAPITAL: Olympia | **POPULATION:** 7,785,786 *(July 2022)*
STATE NICKNAME: The Evergreen State | **YEAR OF STATEHOOD:**
1889 | **FUN FACT:** Washington is the only state to be named after a U.S.
president.

MAIN ATTRACTIONS:

CITIES: Bellevue, Bellingham, Everett, Forks, Leavenworth, Maryhill, Olympia, Pasco, Redmond, Richland, Seattle, Spokane, Tacoma, Vancouver, Walla Walla, Yakima

LANDSCAPES: Columbia River, Ebey's Landing National Historical Reserve, Mount Rainier National Park, Mount St. Helens, Mount Spokane State Park, North Cascades National Park, Olympic Peninsula, Puget Sound, San Juan Islands, Spokane Falls, Strait of Juan de Fuca

POINTS OF INTEREST: Ballard Locks, Chihuly "Bridge of Glass," Chihuly Garden and Glass, Discovery Park, Johnston Ridge Observatory, Lewis & Clark National Historical Park, The Museum of Flight, Museum of Pop Culture, Numerica SkyRide, Pacific Science Center, Pike Place Market, Seattle Art Museum, Seattle Rep, Space Needle, Spokane River Centennial State Park Trail, Stonehenge Memorial, Whitman Mission National Historic Site

DATE VISITED:	WHO I WENT WITH:	WHAT I'D RECOMMEND:
WEATHER:	**FAVORITE MOMENT:**	**TIPS TO FRIENDS/FAMILY:**
WHERE I WENT:		
WHERE I STAYED:	**BEST DRIVING OR WALKING TOUR:**	**WHAT I WISH I KNEW BEFORE GOING:**

WHAT WAS THE FIRST THING I NOTICED WHEN I ARRIVED?

MY FAVORITE PART OF THE VISIT WAS . . .

HOW I SPENT MY TIME THERE:

WHAT WOULD I DO IF I GO BACK?

WHAT IS SOMETHING I LEARNED THERE?

MY TOP THREE FAVORITE ACTIVITIES WERE . . .

1.

2.

3

MY TRIP WAS

JAN   FEB   MAR   APR   MAY   JUN   JUL   AUG   SEP   OCT   NOV   DEC
1   2   3   4   5   6   7   8   9   10   11   12   13   14   15   16   17   18   19   20   21   22   23   24   25   26   27   28   29   30   31

West Virginia

STATE CAPITAL: Charleston | **POPULATION:** 1,775,156 *(July 2022)*
STATE NICKNAME: The Mountain State | **YEAR OF STATEHOOD:** 1863
FUN FACT: People have been living in West Virginia for at least 10,500 years, according to the discovery of ancient spearpoints.

MAIN ATTRACTIONS:

CITIES: Charleston, Harpers Ferry, Grafton, Huntington, Moundsville, Weston

LANDSCAPES: Allegheny Mountains, Blackwater Falls State Park, Blue Ridge Mountains, Cass Scenic Railroad State Park, Cumberland Mountains, Gauley River National Recreation Area, Hawks Nest State Park, Monongahela National Forest, New River Gorge National Park & Preserve, Potomac River, Spruce Knob–Seneca Rocks National Recreation Area

POINTS OF INTEREST: Avampato Discovery Museum, Capitol Market, Clay Center for the Arts & Sciences, Cox-Morton House, Exhibition Coal Mine, Grave Creek Mound Archaeological Complex, Green Bank Observatory, The Greenbrier, Heritage Farm Museum & Village, John Brown's Fort, Keith-Albee Performing Arts Center, Marshall University's Memorial Fountain, New River Gorge Bridge, Philippi Covered Bridge, Ritter Park Historic District, West Virginia State Museum, West Virginia Veterans Memorial

DATE VISITED:	WHO I WENT WITH:	WHAT I'D RECOMMEND:
WEATHER:		
	FAVORITE MOMENT:	**TIPS TO FRIENDS/FAMILY:**
WHERE I WENT:		
	BEST DRIVING OR WALKING TOUR:	**WHAT I WISH I KNEW BEFORE GOING:**
WHERE I STAYED:		

WHAT WAS THE FIRST THING I NOTICED WHEN I ARRIVED?

MY FAVORITE PART OF THE VISIT WAS . . .

HOW I SPENT MY TIME THERE:

WHAT WOULD I DO IF I GO BACK?

WHAT IS SOMETHING I LEARNED THERE?

MY TOP THREE FAVORITE ACTIVITIES WERE . . .

1.

2.

3

MY TRIP WAS

/10

JAN	FEB	MAR	APR	MAY	JUN	JUL	AUG	SEP	OCT	NOV	DEC
1 2 3	4 5 6	7 8 9	10 11 12	13 14 15	16 17	18 19 20	21 22	23 24	25 26 27	28 29	30 31

Wisconsin

STATE CAPITAL: Madison | **POPULATION:** 5,892,539 *(July 2022)*
STATE NICKNAME: The Badger State | **YEAR OF STATEHOOD:** 1848
FUN FACT: The resort town of Wisconsin Dells also boasts the world's largest concentration of water parks and offbeat attractions.

MAIN ATTRACTIONS:

CITIES: Egg Harbor, Fish Creek, Green Bay, Madison, Milwaukee, Mineral Point, Racine, Sheboygan, Spring Green, Two Rivers, Wisconsin Dells

LANDSCAPES: Ahnapee State Trail, Apostle Islands National Lakeshore, Bay of Green Bay, Blue Mound State Park, Brule River State Forest, Copper Falls State Park, Door Peninsula, Hank Aaron State Trail, Ice Age National Scenic Trail, Kohler-Andrae State Park, Lake Superior, North Beach, Pere Marquette State Park, Saint Croix National Scenic Riverway

POINTS OF INTEREST: Chazen Museum of Art, Hamilton Wood Type & Printing Museum, Harley-Davidson Museum, House on the Rock, Lambeau Field, Milwaukee Art Museum, Milwaukee Public Museum, Neshotah Park & Beach, Olbrich Botanical Gardens, Racine Zoo, Rick Wilcox Magic Theater, Top Secret, Unitarian Meeting House, Wind Point Lighthouse

---

DATE VISITED:

WEATHER:

WHERE I WENT:

WHERE I STAYED:

WHO I WENT WITH:

FAVORITE MOMENT:

BEST DRIVING OR WALKING TOUR:

WHAT I'D RECOMMEND:

TIPS TO FRIENDS/FAMILY:

WHAT I WISH I KNEW BEFORE GOING:

WHAT WAS THE FIRST THING I NOTICED WHEN I ARRIVED?

MY FAVORITE PART OF THE VISIT WAS . . .

HOW I SPENT MY TIME THERE:

WHAT WOULD I DO IF I GO BACK?

WHAT IS SOMETHING I LEARNED THERE?

MY TOP THREE FAVORITE ACTIVITIES WERE . . .

1.

2.

3

MY TRIP WAS

10

JAN		FEB		MAR		APR		MAY		JUN		JUL		AUG		SEP		OCT		NOV		DEC
1	2	3	4	5	6	7	8	9	10	11	12	13	14	15	16	17	18	19	20	21	22	23	24	25	26	27	28	29	30	31

Wyoming

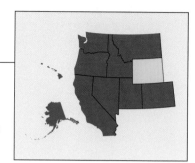

STATE CAPITAL: Cheyenne | **POPULATION:** 581,381 *(July 2022)*
STATE NICKNAME: The Equality State | **YEAR OF STATEHOOD:** 1890
FUN FACT: Devils Tower, a huge volcanic plug, rises 1,267 feet, higher than the Empire State Building.

MAIN ATTRACTIONS:

CITIES: Cheyenne, Cody, Fort Bridger, Jackson Hole, Laramie, Sheridan, South Pass City, Thermopolis

LANDSCAPES: Bighorn River, Devils Tower National Monument, Flaming Gorge National Recreation Area, Grand Canyon of the Yellowstone, Grand Prismatic Spring, Grand Teton National Park, Great Plains, Jackson Lake, Jenny Lake, National Elk Refuge, Old Faithful Geyser, Snake River, Star Plunge, Wind River Range, Yellowstone National Park

POINTS OF INTEREST: American Heritage Center, Cheyenne Frontier Days, Dan Miller's Cowboy Music Revue, Fort Laramie National Historic Site, Fossil Butte National Monument, Historic Governors' Mansion, King's Saddlery, Laramie Plains Museum, Mountain Man Rendezvous, National Historic Trails Interpretive Center, National Museum of Wildlife Art, Nelson Museum of the West, Railroad Heritage Park, Wyoming State Museum

DATE VISITED:

WEATHER:

WHERE I WENT:

WHERE I STAYED:

WHO I WENT WITH:

FAVORITE MOMENT:

BEST DRIVING OR WALKING TOUR:

WHAT I'D RECOMMEND:

TIPS TO FRIENDS/FAMILY:

WHAT I WISH I KNEW BEFORE GOING:

WHAT WAS THE FIRST THING I NOTICED WHEN I ARRIVED?

MY FAVORITE PART OF THE VISIT WAS . . .

HOW I SPENT MY TIME THERE:

WHAT WOULD I DO IF I GO BACK?

WHAT IS SOMETHING I LEARNED THERE?

MY TOP THREE FAVORITE ACTIVITIES WERE . . .

1.

2.

3

MY TRIP WAS

/10

JAN   FEB   MAR   APR   MAY   JUN   JUL   AUG   SEP   OCT   NOV   DEC
1 2 3 4 5 6 7 8 9 10 11 12 13 14 15 16 17 18 19 20 21 22 23 24 25 26 27 28 29 30 31

STATE I VISITED:

DATE VISITED:

WEATHER:

WHERE I STAYED:

WHO I WENT WITH:

FAVORITE MOMENT:

BEST DRIVING OR WALKING TOUR:

WHAT I'D RECOMMEND:

TIPS TO FRIENDS/FAMILY:

WHAT I WISH I KNEW BEFORE GOING:

WHAT WAS THE FIRST THING I NOTICED WHEN I ARRIVED?

MY FAVORITE PART OF THE VISIT WAS . . .

HOW I SPENT MY TIME THERE:

WHAT WOULD I DO IF I GO BACK?

WHAT IS SOMETHING I LEARNED THERE?

MY TOP THREE FAVORITE ACTIVITIES WERE . . .

1.

2.

3

MY TRIP WAS

/10

STATE I VISITED:

DATE VISITED:

WEATHER:

WHERE I STAYED:

WHO I WENT WITH:

FAVORITE MOMENT:

BEST DRIVING OR WALKING TOUR:

WHAT I'D RECOMMEND:

TIPS TO FRIENDS/FAMILY:

WHAT I WISH I KNEW BEFORE GOING:

WHAT WAS THE FIRST THING I NOTICED WHEN I ARRIVED?

MY FAVORITE PART OF THE VISIT WAS . . .

HOW I SPENT MY TIME THERE:

WHAT WOULD I DO IF I GO BACK?

WHAT IS SOMETHING I LEARNED THERE?

MY TOP THREE FAVORITE ACTIVITIES WERE . . .

1.

2.

3

MY TRIP WAS

/10

JAN   FEB   MAR   APR   MAY   JUN   JUL   AUG   SEP   OCT   NOV   DEC
1 2 3 4 5 6 7 8 9 10 11 12 13 14 15 16 17 18 19 20 21 22 23 24 25 26 27 28 29 30 31

JAN	FEB	MAR	APR	MAY	JUN	JUL	AUG	SEP	OCT	NOV	DEC

1 2 3 4 5 6 7 8 9 10 11 12 13 14 15 16 17 18 19 20 21 22 23 24 25 26 27 28 29 30 31

JAN   FEB   MAR   APR   MAY   JUN   JUL   AUG   SEP   OCT   NOV   DEC

1   2   3   4   5   6   7   8   9   10   11   12   13   14   15   16   17   18   19   20   21   22   23   24   25   26   27   28   29   30   31

ACKNOWLEDGMENTS

Thank you to the team at National Geographic Books, especially Gabriela Capasso for gathering all of this journal's useful information and Anne LeongSon for its beautiful design. Also thank you to senior editor Allyson Johnson, editorial assistant Margo Rosenbaum, senior cartographer Mike McNey, senior cartographic research editor Michael J. Horner, senior production editor Michael O'Connor, and production editor Becca Saltzman. And special thanks to Joe Yogerst and the entire team behind the original *50 States, 5,000 Ideas*, which served as the foundation for this journal.

All state populations, as well as the populations of the District of Columbia and Puerto Rico, per 2022 U.S. Census Bureau; American Samoa, Northern Mariana Islands, Guam, and the U.S. Virgin Islands populations per 2023 U.S. Census Bureau.

Since 1888, the National Geographic Society has funded more than 14,000 research, conservation, education, and storytelling projects around the world. National Geographic Partners distributes a portion of the funds it receives from your purchase to National Geographic Society to support programs including the conservation of animals and their habitats.

National Geographic Partners, LLC
1145 17th Street NW
Washington, DC 20036-4688 USA

Get closer to National Geographic Explorers and photographers, and connect with our global community. Join us today at nationalgeographic.org/joinus

For rights or permissions inquiries, please contact National Geographic Books Subsidiary Rights: bookrights@natgeo.com

ISBN: 978-1-4262-2309-9

Printed in China
23/RRDH/1

The information in this book has been carefully checked and to the best of our knowledge is accurate. However, details are subject to change, and the publisher cannot be responsible for such changes, or for errors or omissions. Assessments of sites, hotels, and restaurants are based on the author's subjective opinions, which do not necessarily reflect the publisher's opinion.

SO MANY IDEAS.
SO LITTLE TIME.

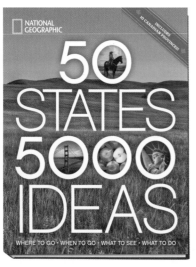

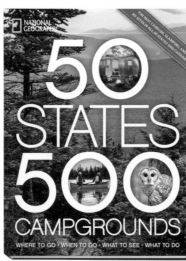